MENTAL MANAGEMENT FOR GREAT GOLF

HOW TO CONTROL YOUR THOUGHTS AND PLAY OUT OF YOUR MIND

DR. BEE EPSTEIN-SHEPHERD

LOWELL HOUSE

LOS ANGELES

CONTEMPORARY BOOKS

CHICAGO

Copyright © 1996, 1997 by Dr. Bee Epstein-Shepherd.

Requests for such permissions should be addressed to:
Lowell House
2020 Avenue of the Stars, Suite 300
Los Angeles, CA 90067

Lowell House books can be purchased at special discounts
when ordered in bulk for premiums and special sales.

Library of Congress Card Catalog Number: 96-84466

ISBN: 1-56565-799-3

Text design: Valley Typesetters, Carmel Valley, California

Manufactured in the United States of America
10 9 8 7 6 5 4 3 2 1

ACKNOWLEDGMENTS

This book is the result of friendships, love, support, inspiration, advice, research, experience, and hard work.

Many have contributed one or more of the above elements.

Thank you to Gerald Kein for introducing me to the Elman techniques. To Dian Murphy, who taught me the fundamentals of golf and continues to support my learning and my work. To Karen Hunter Moraghan for introducing me to many of the people who are also listed here. To those who contributed ideas, read manuscript drafts, provided examples, and in other ways influenced this book: Jane Blalock, Sally Dodge, Shelley Hamlin, Betty Hicks, Bob Hughes, Jim Langley, Richard Moss, Chuck Perry, Bob Shepherd, Laird Small, Don Spencer, Hollis Stacy, Barbara Williams.

Special thanks to Ellison Ferrall, who stimulated me to play my best at writing, and to my ever faithful editor Grace Darcy. To my daughters, Bettina and Nicole, for their love, support, and proofreading, and to my son, Seth, who constantly challenges me to greater achievement and who is responsible for the jacket design.

CONTENTS

INTRODUCTION

PART I: THE MIND

PART II: THE FOUR KEYS TO MENTAL MANAGEMENT

PART III: HOW TO USE THE FOUR KEYS

PART IV: PERFORMANCE BREAKTHROUGHS WITH HYPNOSIS

PART V: HOW TO APPLY THE FOUR KEYS AND HYPNOSIS TO YOUR LIFE

Mental Management For Great Golf:

How to Control Your Thoughts and Play Out of Your Mind

INTRODUCTION

We have all seen golfers who keep their hands on a trophy for fifteen holes only to give it away on the last three. We've watched in agony as tour players collapse in the fourth round after being on top of the leaderboard through most of the tournament. If the weather and course didn't change, the clubs and balls are the same, the swing and stroke are still solid, why does this happen? It happens because thoughts go out of control.

Mental management is the key to winning performance. Professional or amateur competitors must control their thoughts and keep cool under pressure to play great golf. They can do it using the techniques in this book. If you're not a competitor, but play just for fun, you'll have more fun when you hit more fairways and sink more putts. Use my **Four Keys to Great Golf** to manage your thoughts and watch your game reach new heights.

Practice your game physically on the range, putting green, the backyard, and in front of the bedroom mirror. Add mental management, and you'll be able to control your thoughts, play out of your mind, and keep your trophy!

■

I teach mental management to athletes who want to play their best and win. This book focuses on the work I do with golfers. My clients get results immediately, and many need only one or two sessions with me. My very first golf client said, "After only two sessions with Bee, my score dropped from an average of 85 to 80." From another, "After only one session and by consistently practicing in my mind, I have taken nine strokes off my game in six weeks." If you practice only mechanics, you might take months or even years to achieve this sort of improvement. When you add the **Four Keys** to your practice routine, you'll progress very rapidly.

What's so special about these methods? They capitalize on the least utilized source of performance improvement technology–the mind. Jack Nicklaus said, *"Golf is 90 percent mental."* If that's so, *why does the average golfer spend all of his practice time hitting balls, and totally neglect mental management, or 90 percent of the game?*

The answer is threefold:
1. People are not aware of how powerful the mind is, and how much it influences performance in sports, and, for that matter, every area of life.
2. They don't know how to harness and use the mind's power effectively.
3. There's no physical action in mental practice– it's more fun to swing the club and belt the ball.

I deal only with the **"neglected 90 percent"**–the mental aspects of the game. This book will make you aware of how *your mind can stimulate victory or lead to defeat.*

I'll show you how to tap your hidden reserves and allow your body to do what it already knows how to do. (You *do* know how to hit the ball – you've hit plenty of great shots when no one was looking or when you weren't counting.)

■

The mind's impact on athletic performance is well researched. Olympic competitors, professionals, and other elite athletes have their own winning mental techniques. All these techniques have certain elements in common. I have condensed and simplified the best of the mental techniques and developed the **Four Keys to Great Golf**. They are easy to learn, easy to use, and they get results.

For the best results, I recommend that you learn solid mechanics from a good teaching professional. Even experienced touring pros continue to work with coaches who adjust their swings and strokes. Teaching professionals are masters of techniques that produce the best shots. Many have developed unique methods or systems based on knowledge of the body and how it moves, the technology in equipment, the laws of physics, and vast experience working with a wide variety of students. *Learn the fundamentals of golf from the professionals*. Ignore advice from anyone whose handicap is higher than an acceptable basketball score.

Support and enhance what you learn from your professional with mental training. *The right mental training helps you learn more quickly, retain and use more of what you learn, and perform at higher levels whether you compete or play just for fun.*

■

As you use the mental techniques I teach you, you will develop a smoother, more consistent swing and reliable stroke. You will have more composure on the first tee, be able to maintain concentration and focus, make better decisions, improve course management, and three-putt less. As your game quickly improves you'll develop unshakable confidence and have much more fun on the golf course. You'll probably win too!

■

If I asked you why you play golf, you'd probably tell me, "I play for recreation. I want to forget work, relax and just enjoy myself."

At a recent corporate outing, I watched one executive become very frustrated, begin to talk to himself in less than complimentary ways, escalate into real anger, and throw down a club. I wondered if this was how he relaxed and enjoyed himself. I suspect he would have had more fun if he hadn't mishit his first drive. He was so intent upon hitting an impressive drive and looking good that he was tense and anxious as he addressed the ball. The tightness in his jaw was evident as he prepared to muscle the ball. Neither his brain nor his muscles gave him what he wanted, a decent first drive. For the rest of the round, he reacted in a very predictable, high scoring way.

Had he learned and practiced the **Four Keys to Great Golf,** the chances of the first poor shot would have been greatly reduced. Had he mishit anyway, he could have gone on to the next shot with calm composure. He probably would not have hit the embarrassing shot, which he allowed to ruin the rest of the round.

■

Even though many golfers claim they are not competitive and just play the game for fun, everyone is ego involved in playing well. When we are honest with ourselves, we really do want to win, whether it be over an opponent, the course, or ourselves.

As I was taking an early evening walk along the golf course I noticed a friend in the twilight, playing by himself. He told me that he and his buddies had just finished a nine hole skins game. He had put in a dollar a hole. Financial loss $9. The real loss was to his self-esteem. He was so upset at not winning any skins that he came out to practice for the next game.

If you want to win the skin or the pot, or whatever is on the line when you play (in addition to your ego), practice the **Four Keys to Great Golf**. They are easy to learn. I can demonstrate and teach them in about an hour. If you practice and use them consistently they will soon become second nature. You'll find your game will improve faster than if you hit buckets of balls on the range with the wrong mental attitude.

■

Tom Kite, Captain of the 1997 Ryder Cup Team, said, *"I have to spend as much time on the mental side of golf as on the practice range."*

If you are like most golfers, you spend no time on your mental game.

Top professionals work with mental coaches. Players who have the most mental control lead the money list. Corey Pavin, who has worked with psychologist Dr. Richard Coop, has one of the shortest drives on the tour. In 1995, he was number four on the money list, with earnings of $1,340,079. John Daly with the longest drive was number fifty-seven, with earnings of $321,748. He earned most of it winning the British Open. Daly has a stunning drive and exceptional touch around the green, but he doesn't have Pavin's mental management techniques.

■

I believe in four things:
1. I believe in learning golf from a qualified professional.
2. I believe in dedicated practice of all the mechanics: your swing, chipping, and putting.
3. I believe in playing with the right equipment.
4. I believe even more strongly in practicing mental management.

If you want to be a consistent winner, your mind matters more than the size of your body, the power of your swing, your club, or the balls. Mental management assures confidence, focus, control, and your best game. As you read this book, you will understand why.

■

Part I introduces you to how the mind works. After all, if you want to manage your mind, it's helpful to know something about what you are managing.

Each of the **Four Keys to Great Golf** is covered in a general way in Part II. **The Keys** are #1. Relax and Let Go. #2. Think Only Great Shot Thoughts. #3. Visualize: What You See Is What You Get. #4. Practice in Bed.

In Part III, I'll give you specific ideas on how to use the **Keys** to improve your game, increase your confidence, and play your best.

Part IV deals in detail with an advanced mental skill that can cause performance breakthroughs in any area of life – hypnosis.

Hypnosis is the "Great Big Bertha® of the mind." Just as it is possible to play well with a regular size driver, it is possible to play well concentrating just on mechanics. The Great Big Bertha® was considered outrageous when it was introduced, but golfers liked it because it improved their game. Hypnosis for golf is seen as outrageous by many people, but it improves play more quickly than other methods. When people use it, they experience amazing results. Both the Great Big Bertha® and hypnosis raise playing to higher levels.

In Part IV you'll learn what hypnosis is and how it can improve your golf game. Hypnosis is incredibly effective in eliciting winning performance from athletes. Many Olympic teams travel with their own corps of hypnotists. You don't need a hypnotist in tow when you compete. You will learn the basics of self-hypnosis in Chapter 15. When you are able to hypnotize yourself while playing, you can create what I call, the **"zone on command."** This skill can be applied to any situation in which you want to excel.

The last section, Part V, How to Apply the **Four Keys** to Your Life, is an added bonus. Don't limit mental management techniques to golf or sports. The basic concepts are the foundation for the strategies used by highly successful people in their business and personal lives. You can modify and adapt the techniques you learn here to help you perform at your peak and have more satisfaction and joy in every area of your life.

PART I

THE MIND

If you want to be a consistent winner, your mind matters more than the size of your body, the power of your swing, your clubs, or the balls.

When you understand how your mind functions, you can control your thoughts, your game, and your life. In this part, you learn how your mind can either stimulate success or assure failure.

CHAPTER 1

UNDERSTANDING HOW THE MIND WORKS

Preview

The subconscious mind has a greater influence on your golf game than the conscious mind. Though most people think they are logical, rational, and use common sense, it is the subconscious, which is below the surface, that really determines how you will execute each shot!! Dave Pelz, guru of the short game, researched putting for more than twenty years. He says that the break golfers see with the conscious mind is only 25 to 30 percent of the actual break. They line up to and aim at about 65 percent of the break and steer the putt to 85 to 95 percent. Pelz says,"I can only describe it as a fight between your conscious and subconscious minds." Ultimately, the subconscious mind determines the actual shot.

THE CONSCIOUS MIND

You have a conscious mind and a subconscious mind. You think with your conscious mind. *The conscious mind is alert and aware. It is logical. It analyzes,* "It's 326 yards to the pin, there's water to the left, bunkers to the right and in front of the green, the wind is blowing right to left, and I need par on this hole to stay even. Should I go for it, maybe birdie, but risk the water and bogey, or should I play it safe?" *The conscious mind makes decisions;* "I'm going to go for it," then *makes excuses;* "If my partner hadn't coughed as I was swinging, I would have made that shot." *The conscious mind judges.* "What a jerk! If you had played it safe, you wouldn't be in this position now."

The conscious mind has short-term memory and takes the bogey thought and criticism to the next hole. It also remembers that this is the third bogey in a row. Now, the *conscious mind judges again;* "You are so stupid, you under-club every time. When are you going to learn? At this rate, you'll never be club champion." So you see, the conscious mind evaluates, figures things out, makes decisions that seem logical, and rationalizes, criticizes, or blames when something goes wrong. *The conscious mind also calls itself realistic. It does remember when things go right, but* **memory for right seems shorter than memory for mistakes.**

THE SUBCONSCIOUS MIND

The subconscious operates below the conscious mind. It is not logical, it is emotional. It doesn't think, it feels. It doesn't make decisions, it responds. It doesn't analyze or question, it gets instructions from the conscious mind, and it follows those instructions.

The subconscious has a huge storehouse of long term memory. A memory of everything you have ever experienced is locked somewhere in your brain cells. In the 1950s, while Dr. Wilder Penfield, a noted Canadian neuro-surgeon, was performing surgery on a patient, his probe touched a spot on her brain. When this happened, she relived her fifth birthday party. She felt like a five-year-old, talked like a five-year-old, tasted the birthday cake, and remembered the names of the children at her party. She recalled the entire event in vivid detail.

As a result of further research, we know that all past experience is stored in your memory bank and can be recalled. *A memory of every game you have played, and every golf shot you have made is somewhere on a brain cell, just waiting to be recalled.* It doesn't take a surgeon's probe. *The subconscious will bring the information to the surface when it has been given the right instructions.*

The conscious mind thinks, "I need to hit this drive straight down the middle." This thought becomes your instruction to the subconscious mind. The subconscious then searches its vast storehouse of memory, "What does my body need to do to hit down the middle?" It finds the information and carries out the instructions. The process works exactly like a computer. When you give the computer a command, it searches through its huge memory and, almost instantaneously, carries out your commands.

■

Most of us confuse the subconscious with too many conflicting or improperly worded instructions. "I need to hit this drive straight down the middle, but I've been slicing lately. Maybe I'd better aim left. I should have taken my 3 wood instead of the driver. I better not hit it fat. I really need a par here." As you talk to yourself, you give your subconscious too many mixed messages. Result – a mishit.

■

When it's your turn to putt, you read the green, determine the line, address the ball, then give yourself the conscious command, "In the cup." The subconscious hears the simple, clear command and carries out your instructions. If you have practiced putting, the subconscious knows exactly how to direct your muscles to sink the putt. It needs no more instruction from your conscious mind than "in the cup."

Through life experience, the subconscious has developed a keen spatial sense, so your subconscious knows how to give you what you want. (When someone throws you a ball, your subconscious directs your muscles to make the catch. No conscious calculations are involved).

After you have played golf for a while, your subconscious has taken in a great deal of information about greens and stored it in its data base. Left to its own devices, the subconscious would direct far more good putts than your conscious mind allows. If you stand over a pressure putt that really matters and think doubt or fear thoughts, overanalyze, or try to control, you only confuse your subconscious. *The yips are a perfect example of a confused subconscious.*

■

As you learn a new physical skill, the conscious mind is continually thinking. You evaluate, analyze and judge your performance, and make changes or adjustments. An active conscious mind is appropriate as you are learning. Then you practice until the new skill becomes programmed. *Eventually, the new behavior should become so automatic that you no longer need to think about it. You make a conscious decision, "straight down the middle." If you let go of further instructions, the subconscious will direct the body to do what you want.*

■

If you play a musical instrument and practice diligently, you finally memorize a piece. Whenever your conscious mind tells you to play that piece, your subconscious immediately takes over and directs your fingers. You play without looking at the music, consciously thinking about what notes come next, or what your fingers are doing. *The subconscious has been programmed through practice to direct the muscles in an unbelievably complex physical sequence.*

When you learn to play golf, or when you change your swing, you pay attention to what you are doing as you practice. You talk to yourself as your conscious mind gives your body instructions. You focus and concentrate on each shot. You consciously go through the movements over and over until the swing becomes automatic.

Through repetition, your subconscious is programmed to automatically recreate a series of movements in response to a specific swing thought or trigger. After you line up and address the ball, your conscious mind says, "slow and smooth," "to the target," "relax," "easy," or whatever simple swing thought or movement you use. At this point, your subconscious automatically takes over. Instantaneously, it orchestrates all the muscles in your body to produce the shot you want. Hopefully, you have taken lessons from someone who has taught you the correct muscle movements.

■

The subconscious is a creature of habit; it doesn't give up old behaviors gracefully. It struggles to keep the familiar. That's why it takes so long to change a swing by using traditional methods. In 1985, when Nick Faldo first went to David Leadbetter to work on his swing, Leadbetter told Faldo that it would take about eighteen months to two years to get it right. It takes a long time for the subconscious to let go of old programming and habits. In the chapters on hypnosis, you'll learn that mental training and hypnosis will dramatically speed up the process.

■

The most common complaint I hear from my clients is, "I hit great shots when I'm practicing, but the minute I get on the first tee and it counts, I lose it." Why? Because when you are playing, you want to look good, do well, and win. You have expectations, so your conscious mind becomes judgmental, "I really have to hit a good tee shot – I hate to look like a duffer." For good measure, you give yourself additional instructions, "Remember to stop at the top of the backswing, don't be in a hurry to swing. You really hit a miserable shot here last week." Thoughts of doubt and concern enter your consciousness and the subconscious listens. It is now confused. It no longer has a clear set of instructions. When the subconscious mind is confused it searches its memory. The most recent memory is of last week's miserable shot. The subconscious uses that memory as directions for your next shot. You hit another miserable shot.

To play great golf or any other game, you must control your conscious thoughts and give your subconscious simple clear directions.

"But," you say, "I am clear. I tell myself, 'Don't hit into the water.' What could be clearer than that? The ball ends up in the water anyway." One more important point. *The subconscious doesn't understand don'ts.* If you have a dog you have trained to sit, when Rover hears the word sit, he sits. What do you think Rover would do if you said, "Don't sit?" That's right, he would sit. Rover doesn't understand "don't," but the word "sit" is familiar. He has been trained or programmed to respond to that word. Your subconscious doesn't understand "don't" either. So when you tell yourself, "Don't hit into the water," the subconscious hears "water" and says to itself, "Oh, he wants me to give the little white ball a bath."

■

Mental Management involves teaching your conscious mind to give the right instructions to your subconscious.

Your subconscious has stored a lifetime of experiences and "how-tos" in its memory bank. Unfortunately, some of your long held "how-tos" are not helpful. They were pro-grammed incorrectly.

One of my clients, an extremely talented amateur golfer, played very well with the baseball grip her father taught her as a child. She wants to play on the LPGA tour. She found a good teaching professional to reprogram her mechanics. The first thing the pro told her to do was to "get a grip." She succeeded in getting a physical grip. Now, she is working with me to "get a grip" mentally.

During our initial interview, she said, "Whenever I birdie, I bogey the next hole." Apparently, during a past tourna-ment, she bogeyed twice after birdies. Her conscious mind noticed and judged her harshly. She was angry with her-self. *The subconscious responds well to emotion.* Thereafter, whenever she birdied a hole, her next thought was the fear of a bogey. She inadvertently gave her sub-conscious "it's time to bogey now" messages. Her subcon-scious mind directed her body to carry out those instruc-tions. I am teaching her to give useful messages to her subconscious. The **Four Keys to Great Golf** will teach you to give the right instructions to your subconscious.

■

Slumps are another example of incorrect messages direct-ing behavior. Beth Daniel gave herself an incorrect mes-sage after missing the 1981 U.S. Open title by one stroke. She said, "That loss almost destroyed me." Her conscious thought, "You can't win," was a clear message to her sub-conscious to direct her body to play beneath her potential. She lost her confidence for three years.

Sometimes a slump is the result of a major emotional event, such as the loss of a love, a professional setback, or an injury. Sometimes, after a few poor rounds, or a string of missed putts, a player might develop concern about a slump. These conscious doubt thoughts, "I wonder if this is the start of a big S? I know my turn has to come sometime," are emotionally charged and create anxiety. Anxiety and doubt confuse the subconscious.

When confused, the subconscious does the easiest thing. It focuses on the strong familiar word. Slump is a strong familiar word. The subconscious begins to give mixed messages and slump producing instructions to the body. The next few poor shots reinforce doubt, resulting in more tension and anxiety. Now, muscles tighten, and the swing really is off. Unless a player has good mental skills, the slump cycle may begin.

According to Sheila Ostrander and Lynn Schroeder in their book, *Superlearning*, *"As the grandfather of all modern suggestive systems, Emile Coue wrote, 'When the imagination and the will are in conflict the imagination invariably gains the day. . . . In the conflict between the will and the imagination, the force of the imagination is in direct relation to the square of the will.'* **A person who fears losing a sports match has a mental image of failure. The more the will tries to struggle with this image, the more energy the image gains. The 'fatal attraction' of the bunker for the nervous golfer is due to the same cause. With his mind's eye he sees his ball alighting in the most unfavorable spot. He may use any club he likes, he may make a long drive or a short; as long as the thought of the bunker dominates his mind, the ball will inevitably find its way toward it. The more he calls on his will to help him, the worse his plight is likely to be."**

If a golfer has a few bad rounds or misses a few cuts, slump thoughts can enter the mind. The more the golfer struggles with the slump image, the more energy that thought gains.

When you are trained in mental management, you don't give your subconscious messages that create the conditions you fear. You no longer tell yourself you are playing poorly and losing your touch. You no longer imagine or fear the worst, while consciously struggling to play well. Mental management can get rid of old demons, negative programming, doubts, anxieties, slump concerns, and other distracting, performance inhibiting thoughts. As you learn and use the **Four Keys** your conscious mind will give high performance messages to your subconscious, allowing you to play great golf.

WHAT TO DO:

- Learn good basic mechanics from a teaching professional.

- Practice those mechanics to program them into your subconscious mind. Practice during practice sessions, never when you are counting strokes.

- During practice, if you are hitting poorly with a particular club, stop. You don't want to reinforce or program poor shots. If you're using your driver, go to an iron, or putt instead. If nothing is working, quit for the day.

- Learn and practice the mental management techniques in this book.

- Be aware that conscious doubt, evaluation, or control while you are making shots keeps the subconscious from creating the results you want.

- Trust the subconscious; respect its power to achieve your goals.

PART II

THE FOUR KEYS

In this part, I introduce you to the **Four Keys to Great Golf** *– a simple model that anyone can use. The* **Keys** *are based on the research on peak performance and the experience of winning athletes. Use them, they work.*

CHAPTER 2

MENTAL MANAGEMENT KEY #1:

RELAX AND LET GO

Preview

Your body and mind function most effectively when you are in a state of relaxed arousal. Muscles respond with the correct movements, learning is faster, and better decisions are made. Have several relaxation techniques in your repertoire. You'll be able to remain calm at crucial moments and control your thoughts and actions.

"I knew it was over when I saw him standing over it (the ball). He looked very comfortable." Corey Pavin said this about Fred Couples, who holed a $270,000 putt in the 1995 Skins game. Fred won the richest hole in the history of the event.

Peak performance in any activity requires a sense of physical and mental comfort. As a golfer, you know that a smooth, fluid swing is impossible with tension in your shoulders, arms, or hands. In the 1920s Dr. Edmund Jacobson, a well-respected physiologist and the foremost researcher on relaxation, proved that when one has stressful, anxious thoughts, one cannot have relaxed muscles – the kind of relaxation that is necessary for the smooth stroke that makes a $270,000 putt.

Conversely, when the muscles are relaxed, one cannot have stressful anxious thoughts – the doubtful thoughts that send mishit messages to the subconscious. When you are relaxed your mind and body can work comfortably together. *To play great golf, you must be able to relax and let go.*

Relaxing is easier said than done. As a matter of fact, the more verbal directions or instructions you give yourself, the harder it will be for you to relax. Telling or commanding yourself to relax takes effort. Effort is not relaxing. You can relax by learning and using some simple techniques. Relaxing your body achieves two important goals: your movements become smooth and controlled, and you get rid of anxiety.

Chances are you won't be in contention for a $270,000 putt, so let's look at what a smooth, consistent stroke or fluid swing can mean to you. Maybe it's the club championship, or a trophy or prize in a charity tournament. Maybe it's lunch or just a few dollars. Whatever it is, winning is wonderful for your confidence and your ego. You don't have to win officially to win. Winning can consist of having a satisfying, enjoyable day in beautiful surroundings.

The truth is, if you learn to relax and let go, you'll be ahead in many ways. If you want a consistent swing, to maintain rhythm, tempo, and gain speed, you must swing relaxed. Your drives will be longer and true. Your putting stroke will be more reliable, and your score will improve. You'll play up to your physical capabilities and enjoy the game more.

■

I introduced relaxed putting to one of the leading teaching professionals in the country who had developed a marvelous system that he taught his students. "The thing is," he said, "I am a good putter, but at a certain distance, I have problems." It was fairly easy to see that, when putting at that distance, he developed just enough tension to create inconsistency in his stroke. I guided him through a relaxation exercise. He felt an immediate difference. "I feel more comfortable; the stroke feels smoother," he said. Comfort and a smooth stroke are essential for perfect putts.

■

A club in your hands and a ball in front of you should be your signal to just *relax and let go.* When you consciously direct, swing too hard, or muscle the ball, your shots are destined to disappoint you. When I work with groups, I use an entertaining and dramatic demonstration to illustrate the influence of conscious directions on the muscles.

I give everyone a tee to hold between their first finger and thumb. Then, I give them a "pep talk." I tell them to focus on the tee between their fingers and say to themselves, "I can drop it " over and over again. Then I ask them to try to drop the tee. Most people are not able to control the action of their fingers and are unable to drop the tee for several seconds. Those who are able to drop the tee say they dropped it with some difficulty. Their fingers didn't want to open, and there was some forcing and jerking in their movements.

Then, I ask them to firmly hold the tee between their fingers a second time. My instructions this time are, "O.K., just let go." All the tees fall easily. This dramatically demonstrates the increased muscle control we have when we are not giving ourselves verbal instructions and "trying."

When your movements are directed by your subconscious, they are smooth. *Don't tell your body how to move, just tell your subconscious what results you want.*

Do you need another example? Try this. Get a glass, fill it with water and put it on a table. Now say to yourself, "Drink some water," and do it. Put the glass down again. Now tell yourself, "Move your right hand towards the glass. Curl your fingers and close them around the glass. Hold the glass firmly. Now tense your arm muscles and bring the glass to your mouth. Open your mouth, rest the top edge of the glass on your lower lip . . . ." This can get rather ridiculous, can't it? If you actually follow these instructions, you'll probably find the water dripping down your front.

Do you want a drink of water? Do you want to drive your car? Do you want to tie your shoes? Do you want to swing the club or stroke the putt? *Relax and let go.*

■

It is difficult to consciously relax when you order yourself to do so. Imagine yourself in the dentist's office. You've got a paper bib under your chin, a bright light shining in your eyes, and a dentist with an assortment of tools peering and poking in your mouth. Then he says "relax." It's not easy is it? *Verbal instructions to relax do little good unless you have been trained in relaxation methods.*

There are some relaxation exercises in the Appendix. After you practice the techniques, you will know the feeling of real relaxation. After more practice, you will be able to create the feeling of relaxation almost instantaneously. This is a handy skill. Once you have mastered relaxation techniques, you can use them anywhere. As a matter of fact, the relaxation technique developed by Dr. Jacobson was originally used to treat insomnia. If you have trouble sleeping use the progressive muscle relaxation technique in Appendix A.

The relaxation of mind and body are essential to great golf. You've tried to putt with tense muscles, haven't you? It's an invitation to three-putt.

I have had clients tell me, "I can't relax." As soon as they say this, they have given their subconscious the message to remain tense. Actually, they have forgotten how to relax and just need to relearn the skill. Relearn the skill by practicing the relaxation exercises in the Appendix. Before long you will experience more calm, composure, and control on the golf course and in your life.

WHAT TO DO:

- Go to the Appendix and learn to relax by practicing the exercises you find there.

- Do one or more of the relaxation exercises several times a day.

- Have fun, play great golf.

CHAPTER 3

MENTAL MANAGEMENT KEY # 2:

THINK ONLY GREAT SHOT THOUGHTS

Preview

*An old Japanese proverb states: "**Sooner or later you act out what you think.**" Thoughts create reality. You can think yourself happy, sad, fearful, confident. Your thoughts direct the subconscious mind to produce the physical action consistent with your thoughts. When playing golf and thinking about what you don't want – to shank, three-putt, or give the ball a bath – you are likely to shank, three putt, or give the ball a bath. Therefore, keep in your mind only what you want. **Think only great shot thoughts.***

During my first year in college, I read a book titled *Mind and Body, Psychosomatic Medicine* by *Flanders Dunbar, M.D.* It wasn't required reading, but the title interested me, so I borrowed the book from the library and discovered something that became my main interest and the cornerstone of my teaching and career. The book dealt with the impact of the mind and thoughts on physical health. I was fascinated.

Over the years, I read everything I could find on the power of the mind and began to experiment on myself. I became aware of my thoughts and the impact they had on every area of my life. I learned that by controlling my thoughts, I could achieve and have whatever I really wanted, as long as I didn't want something that was totally beyond my physical capabilities. I am 5'1" and physically incapable of being 5'6". I am also physically incapable of bench pressing 300 pounds or running the mile in three minutes. Therefore, I don't think about achieving those goals. I *am* physically capable of improving my performance on the golf course or tennis court. In addition to practicing physically, I put my mind to work. My discoveries were not new. References to the power of thought are found throughout literature and history.

I began my career teaching college management courses and developed an interest in the lives of leaders in business and industry. I studied their success strategies. All exceptional performers, whether in business or sports, say that they outperform the field because they have specific goals and think only constructive goal achieving thoughts. When moments of doubt attack, the achievers quickly change doubt thoughts to thoughts of the desired outcome. They hold in their minds and speak only of success.

■

Over the years I passed on the mental management techniques that I learned to my students and clients. As an avid tennis player, I decided to experiment with my tennis game. Mental management worked. Almost miraculously, my serves became consistent, on target, and completely under my control. A double fault was a rarity! It became second nature to use my mind to determine my actions in all my activities.

When I took my first golf lessons, I learned the basics of the grip, stance, and lining up to the target. I have to thank my first teacher, Dian Murphy, Director of Instruction at Rancho Cañada and Laguna Seca Golf

Clubs on the Monterey Peninsula, for her thoroughness and emphasis on fundamentals. I *had* a simple and effective preshot routine before I even became aware of the necessity for a consistent preshot routine.

As I learned, I applied mental techniques. As a beginner, I was ignorant of all the things that can go wrong with a shot, so I had few doubt thoughts. I had my share of whiffs, but when I actually made contact with the ball, I hit it straight and on target more often than not. The first time my class went out to play a few holes, I really observed mental principals in action.

One of the students hit his first drive into the trees to the left of the fairway. He tried a second ball. The second ball followed the first. He said out loud, "**@@!! I always hit into the trees." He continued beating the bushes with and for his golf balls. After a few holes, I realized that I was the only person who hadn't landed in a bunker. As soon as "bunker" entered my consciousness, my ball found the bunker. I had broken the rule to think only on target "great shot" thoughts. My mind noticed and registered what I didn't want – the bunker. I got the bunker. You will too, when bunker thoughts are in your mind.

■

Jeff Sluman won the PGA championship in 1988. At his next tournament, when he was introduced to applause and stepped up to the first tee, he said to himself, "You'd better not blow this, Mr. PGA champion." The champion hit the ball 30 yards. He had focused his thoughts on not blowing the shot, rather than on his intended target. His subconscious responded to what was on his mind. *To get what you want, focus only on the goal or target. Banish all other thoughts.*

■

A new client said, "I was playing with a group of ladies I didn't know, and I wanted to make an impression. I sure did, – but the wrong one. I whiffed on the first tee, triple bogeyed that hole, didn't do any better on the next and, by the third hole, I knew it was going to be a bad day." Actually, she had set herself up for a bad day. By the third hole, she was thinking, "nothing works" thoughts and, sure enough, that's what her subconscious mind instructed her body to deliver. The lie "nothing works" became the truth.

The truth, before she told herself that nothing works, was that this particular shot didn't work. I instructed her never to say, "nothing works," Instead say, "This particular shot didn't work. The next one, or the one after that will." When you play with the expectation that nothing works, you hold negative thoughts in your mind continually. This not only impacts your muscle function, but it also gives your subconscious the wrong message.

■

A golfer who had been playing for more than thirty years began our opening interview by saying, "Golf is a game played for recreation, but it is the most negative four hours one can experience. All we think about are don'ts. Don't hit left, that's out of bounds; don't leave it short; don't hit right, there's the water." *I told him to change his language and taught him to think and talk about do's.*

His main complaint was that his handicap, which had been 6 a few years ago, was now 14, and he was determined to get it down to 9. He explained to me that he was taking his game completely apart, analyzing every movement and inch of his swing, and putting it back together. He gave himself a year in which to get "the right swing." I suggested that he might look at his thinking. I have no argument with someone wanting to recreate a swing that really doesn't work, but I suspect that putting a little time into mental management would give him faster and longer lasting results.

Payne Stewart found this out when he tried to change his swing after winning the U.S. Open in 1991. He was winless in 1994 and won once in 1995. In 1996, as he returned to his old form, including a loop in his swing, he said, "I learned a lot, but now I'm trying to throw all that out and let the old Payne Stewart come out. He can win. I'm one of the best players in the world." Payne Stewart is taking "great shot" thoughts a step further. He is thinking and saying that he is one of the best players in the world. That mind set is going to do him more good than searching for a mechanical perfection that doesn't exist.

Searching for mechanical perfection actually gives the subconscious unclear instructions and creates doubt and anxiety. This is an invitation to disappointment.

■

One of my new clients was getting ready for an important tournament. I asked him how he usually prepared. He said, "When I play a practice round, I notice the hazards and problem areas and decide how to avoid them." I recommended that he just quickly notice but not consciously dwell on how to avoid the problems. Instead he should decide on the best way to play the hole. Dwelling on hazards and problems brings them to the attention of the subconscious mind. *It is far better to have a winning strategy outlined and to imagine playing the round using the best possible shot each time you step up to the ball.*

■

There is a side benefit to focusing on the great shots that you do want. You get extra physical power with these thoughts. When I present a workshop or speak to a group, I often use a very vivid demonstration of this principle. I ask for a volunteer in the group who has hit both a great shot and a miserable shot that she can remember. I ask the volunteer to hold her dominant arm out in front of her, and then I do a test of neutral muscle strength.

Then, I ask the person to think of and describe a great shot that she has hit. With those great shot thoughts in her head, I retest muscle strength. The increase in muscle strength is always obvious to the volunteer and to the audience. Next, I ask the volunteer to think about a miserable shot. I do another retest of muscle strength. The arm always dramatically shows muscle weakness.

Always, that is, except with one particular volunteer. I was bewildered when the muscles showed the same reaction to both the great shot thoughts and the miserable shot thoughts. When the demonstration didn't work according to plan, I asked the volunteer to describe the great shot she was thinking of. She said, "I had trouble keeping the great shot in my mind." Actually, that failure demonstrated the principle even more vividly than if it had worked the way it was supposed to.

■

I'm going to create a scenario that is probably familiar to you. Then we'll look at how you can use Key #2 to control your thoughts.

As you drive to the golf course for a game with a client, you think about how important this account is to you. You want to make a good impression, but not overshadow the client. More important, you don't want to look like a hacker! Even though you hit a bucket of balls on the range last weekend, you haven't actually played a round lately.

You hope you'll be able to hit a decent shot off the tee, gauge distances well and not underclub, as has been your habit in the past. You realize you haven't practiced chipping or putting in a long time. Doubt thoughts begin to creep into your mind.

You arrive at the course, meet your client, check in, go to the first tee, and get ready to tee off. You take a few practice swings; they feel pretty good. Still, you say to yourself, "I hope I can swing this way with the ball in front of me." A memory of whiffing on this tee flashes through your mind. "I hope I don't whiff this time," you say to yourself.

You step up to the ball, take your backswing, hesitate slightly, and – you guessed it, whiff. "I knew it, I do this all the time." You have now set yourself up for a mediocre, or even poor round unless you change your thinking patterns. "What do you mean change my thinking patterns? I thought that I didn't want to whiff, but I did; now, am I supposed to think whiff and I won't?" No, that's not how it works. Several things happened before you teed off.

1. As you were driving to the golf course, you implanted doubt thoughts in your mind. This increased your anxiety and created physiological stress. Your muscles tightened just slightly, affecting your body's ability to swing freely. You probably didn't feel the same level of tension that you have when you are aware of stress; you might even have thought you were relaxed. However, relaxation and coordination are essential in playing golf. Striking the ball just a fraction off center affects the flight of the ball. It is easy to see that the slightest restriction of the swing will impact your shot.

2. When you said to yourself, "I hope I don't whiff," you inadvertently gave your body instructions to get ready to whiff. When the subconscious mind hears the word

whiff, it pulls up the blueprint of your last whiff, or improves upon it with an imagined whiff.

Great golf thinking focuses only on what you do want, not on what you don't want. Poor shot thoughts or doubts create anxiety and stress and give poor shot instructions to the subconscious. Let go of doubt and think only about the next well-executed shot.

It's not easy to obliterate poor shot thoughts, but with awareness, focus, and practice, great shot thoughts can become the only thoughts that enter your mind. Will you be able to execute the great shot every time? Of course not. Even the pros at the top of the money list hit out of bounds, land in bunkers, overshoot the greens, and three-putt. Will you hit a lot more great shots than you did when you had doubtful thoughts? Without a doubt!

■

It takes an exceptional player to turn a game around mentally unless one has been trained in the technique. Betsy King's first shot in the final round of the Shoprite tournament, which won her a place in the LPGA Hall of Fame, was a 40 yard mishit. She recovered for par on the first hole. It's obvious that she had great shot thoughts in her mind.

"But how," you ask, "do I get rid of doubt and other poor shot thoughts?" *A mental principal states: The mind can only think one thought at a time. Therefore, the only way to rid oneself of an unwanted thought is to immediately create a wanted thought.* A simple technique for making this happen is to think of the word "switch" whenever a negative or unwanted thought comes into your mind; then, switch your thought to a wanted thought. For example, when you notice the water and say to yourself, "There goes another ball," immediately say to yourself, "Switch!"

Then, switch your awareness to your target, turning it away from the water. This will take some conscious monitoring of your thinking processes until great shot thoughts become habitual.

WHAT TO DO:

- Have a goal (target). Expect to hit it. No doubt thoughts allowed!!
- Focus all your attention on the target. Then you won't notice what needs to be avoided.
- Become aware of what you think and what you say about your golf and yourself. Ask your playing partner to signal you whenever you make a doubtful or critical comment.
- Use the signal, "Switch!" to immediately correct or rephrase any negative comments or thoughts.
- Create a list of phrases, memorize them, and use them often. Some suggestions follow:
  - *I'm feeling good, I know how to hit some great shots.*
  - *I'm here to have fun.*
  - *I'm going for my target. My body knows how to hit the right shot.*
  - *If I hit a bad ball, that shot's over. The next one will be better.*
  - *I easily get out of tough spots.*
  - *It's just one shot, I'll make up for it later.*
  - *A bunker is just a less desirable lie.*
  - *The rough is just a less desirable lie.*
  - *The water is the least desirable lie.*
  - *I have holed some great putts.*
  - *Everyone hits a bad ball sometimes, and I make up for the bad ones by hitting some great ones.*
- **Trust your subconscious to know what to do.** Once you have good mechanics, let go of specific instructions before you swing. I use the following: "O.K. subconscious, you know how to make this shot."

CHAPTER 4

MENTAL MANAGEMENT KEY #3:

VISUALIZE: WHAT YOU SEE IS WHAT YOU GET

Preview

"One picture is worth a thousand words." An old cliché, but it's true! When you can attach a picture to your great shot thoughts, and see or feel that shot, the subconscious gets a much better idea of how to direct the body.

The second key – *Think only great shot thoughts* are instructions you give yourself verbally. Visualization, often called imagery, involves turning those verbal instructions into pictures and feelings.

Some people can actually "see" detailed pictures in their minds, but for others visual images are fuzzy. Still others experience sensations in their bodies. Nick Price says that he "sees" the bounce and roll of the ball in his mind's eye before setting up. Shelley Hamlin, LPGA tour player, told me she doesn't see the ball at all, but feels the shot in her body. The vividness or clarity of your pictures is not as important as being able to create what you want in your imagination. *You want a great shot on target.*

Visualization was popularized in golf by Jack Nicklaus. In his book, *Golf My Way*, he explained that he "goes to the movies" on the golf course. He says, *"I never hit a shot, even in practice, without having a very sharp, in focus picture of it in my head. First I 'see' the ball where I want it to finish, nice and white, sitting up on the bright green grass. Then the scene quickly changes and I 'see' the ball going there... the next scene shows me making the kind of swing that will turn the previous images into reality."* He says that only at the end of his movie does he select a club and step up to the ball.

Tony Robbins, consultant to many high achievers and author of *Personal Power* and *The Giant Within* says if you want to succeed, study successful people and do what they do. Jack Nicklaus is the most successful golfer in the history of the game. If he makes a big issue of visualizing before each shot, that must be one of the keys to success in the game. It is; not only in golf, but in all games, including the game of life.

Nicklaus says to see only perfect shots – don't create "horror" films of shots in the sand, water, or out of bounds. This is the same as thinking only great shot thoughts. The pros will tell you that they hit fewer than 10 percent of their shots absolutely perfectly. The average golfer has very few perfect shots to recall, so the natural tendency is to remember a poor or mediocre shot from the past and create a "don't do that again" image. If your repertoire of really great shots is limited, create a fantasy of the perfect shot for you and go for it! Johnny Miller suggest you imagine yourself hitting a shot the way your favorite touring pro hits it.

■

In the last chapter, you learned that thoughts influence your muscle strength. Thoughts create emotions. People think themselves into anger, fear, sadness, happiness, and love. When you add pictures and feelings, thoughts gain even more power to influence the subconscious. Strong imagery adds power to thoughts. Your thoughts begin the process of creating what you want. Visualization, imagery, or fantasy fleshes it out.

■

Arnold Schwarzenegger, well-known actor and former Mr. Olympia used mental imagery and rehearsal to build his amazing body. He said that seeing or imagining the muscle he wanted while working out was ten times more effective in developing that muscle than pumping iron without "seeing" his desired outcome.

Ice skater Rudy Galindo won the 1996 U.S. Figure Skating Championship in the biggest upset in decades. His skating was so spectacular that the crowd was on its feet giving him a standing ovation thirty seconds before he had even finished his performance. After winning he said, "The past week, I could visualize me getting off the ice with the crowd standing for some reason."

Some people don't visualize in "mental movies." Some hear, and some people feel with more intensity than seeing. We learn and experience using all three senses – seeing, hearing, and feeling. Each of us has a preferred style. So when I use the phrase, "What you see is what you get," you might want to substitute, "What I hear is what I get," or as Shelley Hamlin would say, "What I feel is what I get." When I asked Betty Hicks, one of the founders of the LPGA, about her preshot routine she said, " I see it, I feel it, I hit it." She sees and feels.

Laird Small, Director of the Pebble Beach Golf Instruction Program and named by *Golf Magazine* as one of the 100 best teaching professionals in the country, said he has his students "call the shot" before they hit it. This is a technique he learned from David Cook of the University of

Kansas. He explained it to me this way. "I have them describe in detail the flight of the ball and exactly where the ball is going to go." Using that technique, everyone can visualize. If you have difficulty visualizing, try Small's technique. From the tee box, look out at the fairway, choose a specific target (not just "out there somewhere"), and describe to yourself the exact flight of the ball as it soars through the air, lands, and rolls.

Hollis Stacy, three-time Women's U.S. Open Champion, told me, "I shape the flight of the ball in my mind." When I asked her if she actually "sees" the ball, she said, "Yes."

People who use and teach visualization often don't get consistent results because they think that just creating the pictures in their mind is enough. It's not. Dr. Richard Suinn, a sport psychologist who has worked with many U.S. Olympic teams, was the first person in the United States to systematize the visualization process for athletes. When I spoke to him regarding the techniques he uses, he confirmed what I had discovered. *To be effective, visualization must be done in the relaxed state – that is when the subconscious mind is most receptive.*

That's why it is essential to have a technique that helps you to relax quickly whenever you need to. The short preshot breathing exercise in Appendix D is perfect for creating the relaxation you need for effective visualization and good shot-making.

If you have trouble visualizing, the exercises in Appendix E will help you develop the skill in a very short time.

■

An article in the March 1994 *Journal of Applied Sport Psychology* on the use of imagery by athletes points out the relationship between the consistent use of imagery and the level of achievement in a sport. It was found that elite athletes, in a variety of sports, used imagery more than good or average athletes. My own experience confirms that. I worked with a high school baseball team. The only player who continued to use visualization was the best player on the team, who had a goal of playing professionally. He worked with me privately after graduation and is well on his way to a career in baseball.

It was also reported that less than 30 percent of coaches in the study encouraged imagery. The conclusion was that *coaches who focus on physical training and neglect the vital mental component limit the potential achievement of their athletes.* Don't limit your own potential; add mental management to your game.

WHAT TO DO:

- Relax.

- Before every shot, pick out and focus on your target.

- Visualize the flight of the ball with as much detail as possible. Try "calling the shot" to yourself.

- Be still, tune into your body and muscles, then pretend you are taking a perfect practice swing. Feel your body creating the swing or stroke necessary to get your desired outcome.

- Work these steps into your preshot routine.

- If you have trouble with imagery, practice imagining different scenes and events in your mind. Daydreaming is imagery!

- Go to the Appendix at the back of the book where you will find exercises to help you learn and practice the skill of visualization.

CHAPTER 5

MENTAL MANAGEMENT KEY #4:

PRACTICE IN BED

Preview

Correct mental rehearsal of your swing, putting stroke, trouble shots, and upcoming match creates confidence and impresses the desired outcome on the subconscious mind. Muscles actually show activity when only the mind is activated. You can get measurable performance improvement without physical practice.

You don't need to spend all your practice time out on the range to make progress with your game. You can even improve your game in bed. When she was interviewed after winning the Olympic Gold in gymnastics in 1984, Mary Lou Retton said, ***"Every night before I go to sleep, I practice my routine in my head."***

■

In a well documented Soviet experiment, four matched groups of world class athletes were put on training regimens prior to the 1980 Olympics. Group One trained only physically, Group Two trained physically 75 percent of the time and mentally 25 percent of the time. Group Three divided physical and mental training time equally, and Group Four put 25 percent of their training time into physical activity and 75 percent into mental activity. Shortly before the Lake Placid Olympics, the athletes were evaluated. Group One, the group doing only physical training showed the least improvement in performance. *The group that showed the most improvement was the group that did the most mental training.*

At Hunter College in New York, sport psychologist Barbara Kolonay set up an experiment in mental rehearsal with basketball players. The experimental group practiced free throws mentally and showed an average 15 percent improvement as a result of mental practice. Electromyographs were attached to the athletes to record muscle activity while they were practicing mentally. The machines recorded muscle activity that corresponded to the movements practiced mentally.

Dr. Richard Suinn attached electromyographs to the Olympic skiers he was training. He was able to tell from the needle tracings on the graph what part of the ski run they were visualizing during mental rehearsal. The tracings spiked when the skiers were practicing jumps in their minds, and were smooth when the ski run was smooth.

■

If you are a recreational golfer, a few minutes of mental practice a day will improve your performance on the golf course. If you are an amateur or professional who competes seriously, make it a point to schedule mental practice time. Rehearse your swing, chips, and putts and play actual games in your mind.

When my clients are preparing for specific competition, they play the course if possible, and make notes as they go along. They pay attention to areas that might pose a problem and decide exactly how to play that shot or hole. They also note their own thoughts as they play. When the practice round is complete, they determine a strategy for playing that course perfectly for their level of skill.

On audiocassette tape, I verbally guide the clients through the round as they want to play it, including messages of support and motivation to give them confidence. The clients then use the tape to "practice in bed." Listening to the tape over and over is like playing the round over and over. *But in mental practice we hit and reinforce only great shots.*

■

A client who had already won a major amateur championship came to me just prior to another because she had lost her confidence. I told her to play the upcoming tournament in her head. "Oh, I already do that," she said. "The night before every match, I play every hole in my head."

I wasn't surprised, since she had already proven herself a winner. However, I was surprised that she had lost her confidence. By exploring her thoughts and visualizations, we discovered that instead of playing every hole to perfection, she had some "I hope I don't bogey that hole" images. She was not always thinking great shot thoughts. When she played, her bogey images created real bogeys.

She didn't win that tournament because she hadn't given herself enough time for effective mental practice. Her confidence had been low for several months. A week of intense mental rehearsal probably would have restored it. Two days was not enough. *Just as a couple of practice swings isn't going to groove in a swing correction, one or two mental rehearsals isn't going to win a tournament.*

■

As you create the mental rehearsal or "practice in bed" session for yourself, it is essential to incorporate the first three mental management keys. *You must relax so you*

*can concentrate; you must think only great shot
thoughts, or about playing the perfect round for you; and
you must visualize or image to give your body the correct
instructions.*

WHAT TO DO:

- **Imagine yourself executing the perfect swing.**
  Pretend you are a spectator watching yourself
  play. What would you look like? Imagine
  yourself on the golf course, aware of the bright
  green grass. Notice the clothes you are wearing.
  Now, observe yourself taking the perfect swing.
  Swing with your driver and then with your other
  clubs. Practice with all your clubs, especially
  those that have given you trouble in the past.
  Now as you practice, imagine and feel your body
  execute the perfect shot. Do this over and over
  again.

- **Do the same drill with bunker shots.** Always
  think about and imagine the outcome you want.
  Never let yourself recall difficulties. Imagine
  yourself in the bunker, confidently assessing and
  planning your shot. Now, see and feel yourself
  swing, visualizing the ball flying out of the
  bunker onto the green, or even into the cup.

- **Mentally rehearse chipping and putting, and
  practice getting out of tough spots.** Again,
  visualize, imagine, feel each great shot completely.

- **Mentally play a round of golf.** As you relax before going to sleep, imagine yourself playing. Start by teeing off on the first hole and play every shot in the ideal way. (Make sure that you can actually hit the shots you visualize. It's O.K. to stretch it a little, but don't pretend you have John Daly's distance.) I realize that a round takes about four hours. Just rehearse each shot from the time you begin your preshot routine. There's no need to visualize walking or driving the cart. You ought to be able to practice a whole round in less than half an hour. You can also take a few minutes out of your busy day to relax and play a few holes in your mind.

- **Make audiotapes of the perfect golf game.** Describe where and how you would like to hit each shot. See yourself going through every part of the preshot routine and imagine each shot executed perfectly. Create positive feelings about how you play and instill confidence in your subconscious mind to produce the right shots.

- **Go out and have fun playing great golf.**

PART III

HOW TO USE THE FOUR KEYS

*In this part, I want to motivate you to actually use the **Four Keys**. Then, I'll show you how make the **Keys** part of your golfing life. You'll soon have reliable tools for a consistent enjoyable game.*

CHAPTER 6

PREPARING TO PLAY

"Perhaps more than any other game, golf requires mental preparedness. . . . legendary performers were able to mount a mental outlook on the game that provided them with confidence in their ability to play every shot and control their emotions and anxieties." Peter Dye, from *Bury Me in a Pot Bunker.*

Most golfers acknowledge that mental preparedness is an essential element in performance. They are told "set goals, focus on winning, concentrate, have the drive, determination, discipline and will to win. Mental tough-ness is essential."

There is some merit to this advice, but it approaches pre-paredness from only one perspective, that of working or efforting at it. You already know that too much effort pre-cludes good shot-making. Effort, or "I've got to perform," thoughts create anxiety and tension in the muscles. Tom Lehman said it well after three-putting the eighteenth hole and taking himself out of the running for a win at the 1996 Hawaiian Open, "It becomes so important that you make the putt that you tense up and shoot it eight feet past the hole."

Sometimes this tension can be so subtle and deep that you don't even notice it; it might be the way you always feel. There must be a way to become mentally prepared that doesn't require shot destroying effort and tension. There is. It involves using the **Four Keys** prior to playing.

USING THE FOUR KEYS FOR PREPARATION

■ *Relax and Let Go.* First, learn and use your relaxation techniques. These work well to lessen pregame anxiety. Tour players whose hearts pound, knees shake, and stomachs churn are diverting their focus and sapping vital winning energy from their bodies.

One of my clients, a teaching professional, had high levels of anxiety that interfered with her sleep before tournaments and her play during tournaments. When she learned relaxation techniques, she was able to conquer her sleeplessness and had more energy to put into her performance.

■ *Think Only Great Shot Thoughts.* When you think about your upcoming round, think only great shot thoughts. Let go of concern about the course, conditions, your playing companions. Above all do not indulge in comparing your game or yourself with them. Do not relive or think about a previous poor round. Expect to enjoy your outing and expect to play well.

■ *Visualize: What You See Is What You Get.* Build on your great shot thoughts and visualize your desired outcomes. As you mentally rehearse, create in your mind only what you want. Don't allow your mind to create the worst case scenario.

■ *Practice in Bed.* Mentally rehearse your swing and strokes before you play, following the suggestions made in Chapter 5. Then use the generic visualization scripts you will find in Appendix F. Finally, customize your own visualizations.

This type of mental preparedness will allow you to approach the game as an enjoyable, positive experience. It allows no self conscious thoughts of, "I hope I don't make a fool of myself on the first tee," or thoughts of "having to perform or look good." I'm not suggesting that you give up your competitive spirit and healthy desire to do your best. I am suggesting that you maximize your skill and play up to your potential. The **Four Keys** will give you the mental strategies to do that.

In Appendix F you will find a visualization for developing the conditioned response of relaxed confidence. Relaxed confidence is a shortcut to great golf.

CHAPTER 7

OVERCOMING FIRST TEE JITTERS AND PERFORMANCE ANXIETY

When Betsy King made it into the LPGA Hall of Fame on a 40 yard mishit off the first tee in the final round of the 1995 Shoprite Classic it was because she put the importance of the first tee shot into perspective. It is only one shot. That's all. On a par 72 course it totals only 1.4 percent of the shots. The first tee, or as a matter of fact, the drive off any tee does not determine the outcome of the match. You can always recover from a mediocre or even miserable drive. You cannot save the hole after a three-putt.

Why are we so nervous or anxious on the first tee? After all, we get seventeen more chances to tee up. On the first tee, most golfers are more concerned with how they will look to others than with the final score. Jeff Sluman's mishit on the first tee after his PGA win was undoubtedly a result of his need to maintain an image as a major winner. In golf, the winner is not the player who hits a spectacular opening drive. The winner is the player who has the lowest score at the end of eighteen holes.

■

In 1995, John Daly had the longest drive on the tour. He is exciting to watch. However, on the money list, he finished fifty-three places and a million dollars behind Corey Pavin, whose drive is one of the shortest on the tour. You don't go to the bank with a long drive. The score in golf is the number of total strokes and, for professionals, the amount of money won. Hopefully, this puts the importance of the first tee and a long drive in perspective. The short game is far more important that the first tee Why don't we talk about "from 100 yards jitters?" *Actually, what happens from 100 yards in on the back 9 is far more important than the first tee.*

Sure it's fun to hit long drives. It gives one a sense of power, and strength. If you want the thrill, then get involved in driving contests; see how far you can hit on the driving range. On the golf course go for the numbers that count. Thinking "let's see how far I can hit this," or "I'd better not embarrass myself," automatically sets up performance anxiety. Your muscles tighten and your swing is restricted. These are not the circumstances that make for great golf.

USING THE FOUR KEYS TO OVERCOME FIRST TEE JITTERS

■ *Relax and Let Go.* This is crucial. Anxious thoughts and muscle tension go together. When you do relaxation exercises as preparation for play, your muscles will loosen so you can swing freely. Relaxed muscles eliminate anxiety. You'll step up to the first tee, or any shot, with more confidence.

■ *Think Only Great Shot Thoughts.* When you think doubtful or anxious thoughts, not only do you increase muscle tension, you also create muscle weakness, as I discussed in Chapter 3. Often my clients tell me, "If I don't start off hitting well, I'll look like a hacker." My unorthodox response is, "So what?" You have many other skills, talents, and abilities. If you feel good about yourself, you can let go of your concerns about looking like a hacker.

Helpful thoughts are those that put the importance of one shot into perspective. A poor shot off the first tee is not going to matter – unless your response to that shot ruins the rest of your round. *With that in mind, think, "I know how to hit a good drive," and let your subconscious scan its memory for the mechanics needed to let you do that.*

■ *Visualize: What You See Is What You Get.* Visualize a great tee shot. Use the visualization strategies you learned in Chapter 4. Make sure that the image or picture of the shot you want supports your dominant thought, "I know how to hit a good drive." Visualize and feel yourself going through the motions. You will get the shot that you hold in your imagination.

■ *Practice in Bed.* Mental rehearsal is a wonderful tool for first tee jitters or performance anxiety. Before you go to sleep, and at times during the day when you can relax a few minutes, mentally transport yourself to the golf course and visualize yourself hitting the shot you want – over and over. Get it right in your mind; never create an "I hope I don't do that" image by worrying about mishits. There is a generic visualization script for you to use in Appendix G.

CHAPTER 8

DEVELOPING CONCENTRATION AND LASER FOCUS

Greg Norman missed his chance to win the 1994 PGA Championship when he lost his concentration on a par 5 after a "fan" screamed at him, "You the man!" Flinching at that point is a natural response. A resulting poor shot is understandable. Norman's problem was that his broken concentration went with him to the next shot, and he bogeyed the hole.

Michelle McGann was distracted enough by a twenty minute delay on the fourth tee to give up her comfortable lead at the 1995 Big Apple Classic. That lapse in concentration and focus cost her about $60,000.

Distractions, interference, and lack of concentration are simply other ways of saying you have lost control of your thoughts. You are not focusing your thoughts on making the best shot possible, and your subconscious mind is not getting clear, correct instructions to produce the results you want. *When the conscious mind is pulled to non-productive thoughts, the subconscious follows along – and so does the body.*

I do not know what was on Norman's mind when he bogeyed that par 5, but let me guess. "That jerk! Doesn't he know better than to yell in the middle of a swing. I need to birdie or at least shoot par on this hole. I want this major so badly; I had a real chance until now." This type of thinking fills the mind and dilutes concentration. Keeping focus under these distracting conditions takes skill and energy. The **Four Keys** provide the skill. You just have to provide the energy.

When Michelle McGann suffered her twenty minute delay, I suspect she was thinking thoughts like, "What's the matter with you slow players; this is going to throw my rhythm off. I hate playing at this pace." Had she used the **Four Keys**, the delay could have been used to her advantage.

USING THE FOUR KEYS FOR CONCENTRATION

■ *Relax and Let Go.* Once more I emphasize that when muscles are relaxed one cannot think anxious thoughts. Anxious thoughts produce the wrong focus. Anxious thoughts also produce muscle tension. In Norman's case, the crucial shot was not his tee shot, but his second shot. It hit a tree, probably because there was imperceptible muscle tension limiting the natural flow of his swing. He did not recover from the interference. The correct mind set would have made recovery possible.

Had McGann used some of the waiting time to relax her muscles, her mind would have let go of anxious or non-productive thoughts. She also could have used the waiting time practicing Key #4, mental rehearsal. Before going to Key #4, let's look at how Key #2 can be used to maintain focus and concentration.

■ *Think Only Great Shot Thoughts.* When Norman was originally distracted by the unruly spectator, he could have said to himself, "Switch!" and followed it with, "I can make this up on the next shot; after all, this is a par 5." He could have recalled in his mind a previous successful shot. *When you notice your mind focusing on distractions or interference, immediately refocus and concentrate on what you want – a great shot.*

If you have trouble refocusing, try this exercise. *Stare at an object, such as a ball, a club, or something on the course, maybe the fluttering of the flag, or even blades of grass. Focus on the object and notice things about it. Notice the color and lettering of the brand name on the ball. Notice the pattern of the dimples, the brightness of the white. Does the ball have any scratches or other markings on it? As you focus on the ball, you regain concentration. You can also do a focus exercise as you walk down the fairway. Notice the variations of the grass, the foliage, the clouds in the sky. Verbally describe what you see to yourself. Now transfer that level of focus and concentration to the here and now of making the shot.*

■ *Visualize: What You See Is What You Get.* This key is especially useful for maintaining concentration and focus. Visualizing or creating pictures of what you want in your mind automatically shuts out distractions. You can prepare a good visualization in advance. You might decide, for example, that from now on, *any time a noise, movement, a comment by a partner, or anything else distracts you, you will immediately create a picture in your mind of the ball rolling into the cup.* Since visualizing does take some concentration, you are creating exactly what you need – a focus on your desired results.

■ *Practice in Bed.* You have already figured out that you don't actually have to be in bed to mentally rehearse. You can do it anywhere. It would have been so much better if Michelle McGann had welcomed the twenty minute delay as an opportunity to play a few holes in her head with the ideal outcome, instead of being distracted and disturbed by the slow play. She could have used the time to hone her concentration and focus skills. You can do the same when you are distracted by slow play.

CHAPTER 9

MIND OVER PUTTER

You and your putter determine whether you birdie, par, or double bogey. If you hit a good drive and approach shot, you probably have put yourself in a favorable position on the green. Now, what do you do with that position? If I "named names" of pros who hit the greens in regulation and then bogeyed or worse, I would use up the whole chapter. All you have to do is watch tournaments to know that putts are the shots that make the difference between winning and tying for third – or making the cut. Lets look at how much money is involved.

In the 1995 World Series of Golf, Greg Norman, in a sudden-death playoff, came away with $360,000. Nick Faldo and Billy Mayfair, who also shot 278 during the tournament, had to be satisfied with $176,000, or *$184,000 less.* When there is that kind of money on the line, nerves are tight. The player who can relax and let go has a much better chance of winning.

A tour player can earn more than $100,000 in a tournament by shaving one stroke off his score. I think that kind of potential gain is worth looking at. *Since half our shots are putts, we have the greatest potential to impact our game by improving our putting.* Eliminating mental errors that affect the physical execution of the shot is the easiest and most reliable way to do that.

The putting stroke is the easiest movement in golf. Take the putter back and stroke through on a straight line. *The fewer body parts that have to move, the fewer the potential errors.* Why does something that straightforward create such agony on the golf course? Probably because the putting stroke is so simple. We miss it because we make it too difficult. At the crucial putt, we are at our emotional peak, the most likely time to have uninvited tension in our muscles.

As I talk about the ease of the putt, I don't mean to suggest that there aren't many factors that interfere with holing the ball. I know that the variations built into the greens makes golf more challenging. But in this book we are not talking about how to handle break, speed of greens, and other physical factors. We're dealing only with the mental factors that interfere with holing the ball. *When you're down to the last make or break holes, your ability to control your thoughts determines the outcome.*

I putted better before I knew how. One of my first golf lessons involved lining the putt up with the hole. My pro hadn't yet mentioned break, speed of the greens, or the way the grass grows. I just lined up and visualized the ball rolling into the hole. It often did. Then, I learned the finer points of putting. I learned to read the green. I got drills on speed and distance and break. What I found fascinating is that the more information I tried to process consciously, the more stilted and self conscious my putting became. The more I thought about "having to make the putt," the more often I missed.

The more we process information consciously when we are over the ball, the more confused the subconscious – which directs our muscles – becomes. Process information before you set up. Then let the subconscious take over and sink the putt. When I use the **Four Keys**, my subconscious takes over and does a better job than I can do on a conscious level. Your subconscious will do the same for you.

USING THE FOUR KEYS FOR PERFECT PUTTS

■ *Relax and Let Go.* An article in *Golf Digest* magazine dealt with Tom Watson's yips. In his interview, Watson talked about his nerves, the tight, taut feelings in his body, and his lack of rhythm. He also said that his putter gets off track when it shouldn't get off track. All are interrelated. When there is tension in the body, the stroke cannot be smooth. And when the mind is anxious, or even busy, there is extra tension in the muscles.

During my group mental management sessions, I often set up a putting contest. Then, I put the participants through a relaxation exercise so they can have the experience of total muscle relaxation. After the relaxation exercise, I have a second putting contest to give the participants immediate feedback on the effects of relaxation on putting. They are always impressed by the difference. Since there is no constricting tension in the muscles, the stroke feels smoother and more fluid, and it doesn't get pulled off line. When muscles are relaxed, anxious thoughts are blocked. Then it is easier to focus on "great shot" thoughts, visualize and trust the subconscious.

■ *Think Only Great Shot Thoughts.* Tom Watson is quoted as saying, "I think more about missing a putt than making it." And when he was asked, "What goes through your mind standing over a three footer?" his answer was, "Not the right thing." That's obvious to me because of his well known putting slump. He is getting what he thinks about; "not the right thing."

Calvin Peete once said, *"I never really dreamed of making many putts. Maybe that's why I haven't made many."*

Expectations of making the putt are the only thoughts that should go through your mind. As you read the greens, expect to make the putt. Then, line up and expect to make the putt. Your subconscious is primed to give you what you want – the sound of the ball as it hits the bottom of the cup.

You can only expect to make the putt if you have learned and practiced good mechanics. You also need a consistent preshot routine. When you have these two essentials, thinking the great shot thought and telling yourself, "Into the hole," will give you the best chance at holing your putts.

- **Visualize: What You See Is What You Get.** Lillian's father, an avid golfer with a 4 handicap, was teaching his little girl to play. She had also had several lessons in a junior clinic. Her father said she had a good swing, but her putts were "all over the place." I thought it would be interesting to try my mental techniques on a seven year-old child, who didn't know anything about the "finer points" of putting. When we went out to the green, her father put down some balls. I told her to putt the way she had been taught. Dad was right, the putts were "all over the place."

Then, Lillian and I went into a huddle, leaving Dad on the sidelines. Less than five minutes later, I put down some balls, and asked Lillian to putt. Her astonished father said, "I wish I had a video of the before and after. I've never seen such a dramatic change."

I took just a few minutes to teach Lillian to visualize. Children have wonderful imaginations and can "see" things that don't exist. So I knew that she could probably visualize vividly. We made up a mental game for her. I told her to line up the way her daddy had taught her, and we played the mental game of watching the ball roll into the hole. Then, she was to tell her putter to make the ball go in the hole. Shortly thereafter, at the age of seven, tiny Lillian won her first tournament, beating some eleven-year-olds.

Visualizing involves making up your own mental game. *The essential element of the mental game is to imagine the ball going into the hole.* Some people visualize the ball rolling down an imaginary white line. Others see a very large hole and the ball rolling toward it. I imagine a gold hook on a gold elastic thread coming out of the hole, grabbing the ball and pulling the ball into the hole as the elastic contracts. Sometimes, the more outlandish the picture, the more it holds the attention of the subconscious mind.

■ *Practice in Bed.* Tom Watson continues to work physically at putting, and he does well on the practice green. Earlier in his career, he was an outstanding putter. It's obvious that his body knows how to putt physically; he just doesn't know how to putt mentally. He should incorporate the first three keys into a good routine. Then he should mentally practice that routine over and over. You can do the same. A generic putting script for mental rehearsal is included in Appendix I.

CHAPTER 10
CONSISTENT
CONFIDENCE

"I didn't realize how much confidence means in this game until I didn't have any." Bob Tway, after breaking a five year winless streak.

Confidence breeds confidence. But how do you get it when you have been playing poorly, missing the cuts, or as a recreational player, "hitting into nature" – trees, water, and sand. As a client said, "I am confident, confident that I can't putt." You already know that the conscious messages you give yourself are taken literally by the subconscious. Every missed putt confirms your negative assessment and chips away at your confidence. The opposite is also true. If you notice the putts you do make, and if you give yourself encouragement for your progress, you are moving towards confidence.

Consistent confidence is easy once you recognize that there are factors that interfere with playing your best. The wind, weather, and other people's behavior are out of your control. *Your thoughts are within your control.* Chip Beck, who, with his partner, John Cook, turned the 1993 Ryder Cup around for the U.S. said that positive thinking can turn a mechanical breakdown around. He is so right!

■

Henry Ford said, *"If you think you can, or if you think you can't, you're right."* "But," you might argue," I haven't hit a drive in the fairway in weeks, and I am still shooting in the three figures. If a three-putt is a desired goal, because at this point I'm putting four, the truth is, I'm a lousy player." No, you're not a lousy player! You just haven't developed enough skill yet. *My favorite positive phrase is "I am a developing player."*

To create confidence as a developing player, or to get confidence back if you are in slump, let your imagination come to the rescue. Begin to "fake it till you make it." Pretend you are good. Act like you are good. A method actor becomes the part he is playing. You can become a method actor on the golf course. Your behavior and physiology – how you walk, the expression on your face, the set of your shoulders all impact the way you feel. Hollis Stacy told me that, when she is winning, she walks differently. I told her to start walking like a winner all the time. Her confidence level went way up.

Try this exercise: *Sit down, slump over with your elbows on your knees and your head in your hands. Support the weight of your head with your hands on your forehead. With your eyes closed, slowly rock back and forth.* Do this for about thirty seconds. How do you feel? You probably feel rather down and depressed.

Now, you're ready for the second part of this demonstration. *Stand up straight, put a great big smile on your face. With your hands making fists, throw your arms up as though you have just holed a birdie putt for a trophy and a big check.* Now how do you feel? What changed? Only your physiology – the position and movements of your body.

You can create the feelings you want. You can learn to create feelings of confidence by acting confident – not arrogant, confident. These feelings will influence your subconscious to move you in the direction of your desires. First, create a confident physiology. Stand straight. Shoulders square, eyes straight ahead, head high, and put a smile on your face. Breathe slowly, deeply, and deliberately. You feel stronger and more confident already, don't you? When you play with this physiology and method act confidence, you will hit better shots, creating the basis for genuine confidence.

USING THE FOUR KEYS FOR CONFIDENCE

■ *Relax and Let Go.* Make sure you do relaxation exercises often. Relaxation reduces the anxiety that can wipe out confidence. Do relaxation exercises before you play. Do preshot breathing before you swing.

■ *Think only Great Shot Thoughts.* The moment you even consider thinking negative, poor shot thoughts – Stop! Switch! Recall a great shot! If one doesn't come to mind easily, pretend you have hit one. Remember. Sooner or later, what you think about becomes reality. Focus your attention on the reality you want.

■ *Visualize: What You See Is What You Get.* In your mind's eye, in your body, and in your emotions, create the great shots you want. Imagine yourself striking the ball confidently, with the expectation that the shot will hit your intended target. Feel the power of the swing, and the exhilaration that results when the ball soars through the air.

■ *Practice in Bed.* Appendix G is a mental rehearsal script you can use to develop confidence. Record it on an audiocassette tape and listen often. Or read it over and over until you are familiar with it and can reproduce it in your mind.

PART IV

PERFORMANCE BREAKTHROUGHS WITH HYPNOSIS

Top athletes worldwide rely on an advanced mental skill, hypnosis, to play to their potential. In this part, I show you how you, too, can get amazing composure confidence and performance breakthroughs using hypnosis. **Hypnosis is a heightened state of consciousness in which the mind accepts appropriate suggestions for behavior change.**

CHAPTER 11
HYPNOSIS: PLAY TO YOUR POTENTIAL

"I know hypnosis works, I used it thirty years ago when I was on the tour." Jim Langley, Head Professional, Cypress Point Club, Pebble Beach.

When one of his students asked Langley if she ought to come and see me, he encouraged her. The student was a very serious golfer who had been playing for more than thirty years. She had been taking lessons from the best and playing several times a week, but she had a handicap of 19. When she came to see me, she said she was happy with her mechanics, but her mind kept her playing far below her abilities. She gave me her list of mental errors and showed me the books she was reading to overcome them. I told her that, if she had been taking lessons from the best and playing so often, I had a feeling she already knew everything she needed to know. "Yes," she said, "that's true, but when I get out on the golf course, I can't do it. I just don't have that trust."

I guided her into hypnosis and made suggestions that she trust her swing. I told her that she would notice some improvement in her game after the first session. She might have a lower score, or a better quality of shot, or her outlook, attitude and confidence level might improve considerably. (The subconscious decides what improvements to make first.) I told her that her goal of a 15 handicap would probably take a few sessions, but if she had the shots in her, it could be done more quickly than with physical practice. She said she did have the shots. Jim Langley, her pro, agreed.

When I work with a serious client who is taking lessons, I always speak to the teaching professional to get an unbiased assessment and to support what the teaching pro is trying to accomplish. Langley assured me my client had a fine swing, and with her good putting stroke, there was no mechanical reason for missing putts and playing below her potential. We decided that the first session would concentrate on trusting her swing. We would work on putting during the second session.

She called me two days after her first session. "I just got off the golf course," she said. "I couldn't play all 18 holes because of the condition of the course but in 9 holes I was only 6 over. If I had played 18 I know I would have shot 6 under my usual score. For years pros have been telling me to trust. I've been telling myself that, too, but I never could do it. For the first time, I know what it means, and I did it. I even made a birdie putt with confidence and, when I did miss putts, they were close. I have never putted so well in my life. What a dramatic improvement!" We hadn't even worked on putting, but her subconscious wanted that to improve!

I did work on putting first with another client. He told me he had a one handicap and, in two years, would be eligible for the senior tour. He was considering going for it, but had serious panic attacks on the putting green. "Not always," he said, "but I never know when one will hit." He had talked to a sport psychologist several times and had gotten some advice on relaxing and confidence. He practiced putting an hour every day, but in competition, the panic attacks continued.

I hypnotized him. Because of the nature of these panic attacks, I told him he should be prepared for two or three sessions. After only one session, the panic attacks disappeared. Six weeks later, he told me he had won two tournaments, winning prizes valued at four times what he paid me. It is now a year later, and he is a happy golfer.

Even though she had eighteen tour wins, including four major tournaments, Hollis Stacy had a few subpar years and a loss of confidence. When I worked with her, she told me that when she saw her name on the leaderboard, something happened, and she tightened up. Then, predictably, she fell off the leaderboard. This is a problem common to many players. Six weeks later, at the Nabisco Dinah Shore Tournament, she said to me, "Seeing my name on the leaderboard (where it stayed all four days of the tournament), didn't bother me a bit." I reminded her that one of the hypnotic suggestions I made was that her name belonged on the leaderboard and she would no longer be bothered by seeing it there. Actually, she would be pleased and take it in stride. She finished that tournament just three off the lead, her best finish in more than two years.

■

I see many of my clients only once. A loss in confidence is their most common complaint. They hit decent shots on the practice range and putting green, but their good shots fail them on the golf course. Since hypnosis works extremely well for instilling confidence, many clients are satisfied with their initial results. The clients I see more than once are those who really want to improve their games significantly, and those who compete. It takes more than one session to hone a game to perfection!

One of my clients is serious about winning a major amateur championship. He came to me just before a very important tournament. He wanted to qualify. He did. Because his goals go beyond that particular tournament, we'll be working with his teaching pro to help him reach his ultimate goal. His pro endorses hypnosis as a useful tool.

Do I hypnotize all my clients? No. Why not? Many people I talk to think hypnosis is cheating. It's too easy. Recently a young woman called and canceled her appointment. She said, "What you are telling me seems too easy. I think I should have to work harder to improve." (Before making the appointment, we had a long phone conversation. She told me she had already been working on the game for fifteen years and was at a standstill. Someone suggested to her that she see me.) I told her that, if effort was her criterion, she was welcome to keep efforting, and when she was tired of the struggle, I'd be glad to work with her.

Her attitude was typical of many people. "If it's fast and easy, it must be cheating or gimmicky. If someone is hypnotizing you, improvement is not real, it's just in your mind." The truth is golf is 90 percent mental. *Ken Venturi said, "After you get the basic abilities down, it's all mental."*

Conscious "talk therapy" can help you "change your thoughts," but it takes a lot of time and energy. *Hypnosis is much faster – and it is the only way to get rid of an unwanted "past history."*

It is "past history" that keeps you double bogeying the same hole every time you play it, or always playing a mediocre first round or, worse, collapsing when you're too far ahead. *Hypnosis can help you create a new "past history," a history of success and confidence.* When I work with a player who is in a slump, I have that person relive their wins in hypnosis. This brings their positive history to the foreground and covers over the unwanted past history. This technique is very effective in eliminating doubt and anxiety, creating confidence, and bringing back the winning shots.

■

Many people don't try or trust hypnosis because of fear. To the uninformed, hypnosis is a scary word. It implies "voodoo," loss of control, and being "under the hypnotist's spell." Unfortunately, the only exposure to hypnosis that most individuals have is movies, T.V., or stage shows. A "powerful" hypnotist directs the behavior of the poor "victim" and makes him look like a fool in public. However, people who volunteer for stage shows are generally willing to do silly things to entertain others even when they are not in hypnosis.

Stage shows detract from and dilute the positive potential of hypnosis. When people are comfortable with me as a professional, I ask if they are interested in harnessing the positive power of hypnosis to achieve their goals. Then, they think to themselves, "If this conservative, credentialed person, who doesn't look or act weird, considers hypnosis a useful tool, maybe the sensational aspects actually are entertainment or media hype."

■

Amazing results can be obtained using hypnosis as a constructive tool. Tools are used to create, change, fix, or remodel things. Hypnosis can change, fix, or remodel many aspects of one's life. It was endorsed by the American Medical Association as early as 1958 as a useful technique to reduce or eliminate pain and for other medical and dental applications.

The first wide use of hypnosis was on the battlefield for emergency surgery or amputations when anesthetics were unavailable. Today hypnosis is commonly used to eliminate unwanted behavior, such as smoking, overeating, or procrastination. It can fix behavior that doesn't work, such as discomfort with public speaking, or hesitation about making cold sales calls. It can eliminate phobias, such as fear of flying, needles, or insects. Hypnosis can remodel behavior that works, but could work better. It improves confidence, self-esteem, memory, study habits, and concentration. My favorite use of hypnosis is remodeling behavior in sports.

An athlete who knows how to play the sport, but would like to reach full potential, can do it more rapidly with hypnosis. *Hypnosis relaxes the body, enhances focus and concentration, eliminates performance anxiety, doubts, fears, negative thinking and unleashes the athlete's full physical power.* Research shows that the exhausted athlete recovers from excess exertion more rapidly when using hypnosis as part of the training program. Hypnosis also helps beginners learn more quickly.

CHAPTER 12

THE TRUTH ABOUT HYPNOSIS:

DISPELLING THE MYTHS

Let me dispel the myths surrounding hypnosis. When you let go of misconceptions, concerns, and fears, you can benefit from the positive power of hypnosis. When you understand hypnosis, you might want to make use of this remarkable tool that can enhance your life considerably.

The following are questions that people ask me most often. They're probably the same questions you have, but don't know whom to ask!

- **Are you going to have power or control over me?** No. *I have no power over you. I am your guide to help you do what you are willing or want to do.* Have no concern about looking foolish or saying something embarrassing or telling "secrets." *You are aware and in complete control at all times.*

Volunteers for stage shows look like they are under the control of the hypnotist, but they are not. They remain in control; they're just letting go of inhibitions because they are willing to be entertaining. If the stage hypnotist should make a suggestion that the volunteer would find morally objectionable, or embarrassing, he just wouldn't do it. If I, or any hypnotist, make a suggestion that you don't like or that is not right for you, you just won't do it. Let me say that again for emphasis. *You will never do anything in hypnosis that you wouldn't be willing to do in*

The Truth About Hypnosis: Dispelling the Myths 75

the non-hypnotic state. You'll accept only the suggestions you want to accept. Not long ago, a client asked if I could hypnotize his wife to stay away from Nordstrom Department Store. The answer was, "No – not unless she really wants to stay away."

- **How will I feel when I am hypnotized?** You can find out by closing your eyes for a minute or two and focusing on how your body feels. Then, open your eyes. Many people feel just like you felt with your eyes closed. Some people feel light, tingly and floaty. Some feel heavy and lazy. One client said, "I felt warmth coming over me." Another said, "I feel like I'm in an aura." You might feel any or all of these feelings. Whatever you feel will be comfortable for you; you'll enjoy it. Almost universally, people tell me they are more relaxed than they have ever been – they love the feelings, during and afterward. Everyone I have worked with looks forward to experiencing hypnosis again.

When you are in a hypnotized state, you will be aware of everything that is going on and hear everything the hypnotist says. **You probably won't believe you are hypnotized.** You are able to carry on a conversation in hypnosis. If you hypnotize yourself, you will hear and be aware of everything that is going on. However, what is going on around you won't affect or distract you in any way. Your subconscious mind is in complete concentration and focus, open to desired suggestions without the interference of your critical doubting self. This is very handy on the golf course. **You can learn to hypnotize yourself at will and be totally unconcerned with spectators, the habits of your playing partner, or any of the other distractions that can interfere with your best performance.**

■

When an athlete is playing "in the zone" he is in actually in a state of hypnosis or "waking trance." Bobby Jones once said his iron play "was so exceptional, I felt I must have been hypnotized." He was. He hypnotized himself, but didn't know it.

More than twenty years ago, Michael Murphy, the author of *Golf in the Kingdom*, said Jack Nicklaus was playing in a trance much of the time. You have probably felt that way upon occasion. In his book, *A Good Walk Spoiled*, John Feinstein says, ". . . the game won't let you decide when you will hear the muse. It comes and goes, often for reasons you can't understand or explain." *Hypnosis is the ability to put yourself in the state in which you can hear the muse more often.* When you put yourself in the **"zone on command,"** you can have more control over every aspect of your life.

■ **What happens if I don't wake up or come out of hypnosis?** I don't know – it's never ever happened in the history of hypnosis. Actually, I do know. You'll be studied by experts from all over the world, written up in medical journals, appear on the news, and be on the cover of the *National Inquirer*.

■ **Can everyone be hypnotized?** Yes. Have you ever been so wrapped up in movie or T.V. program that you blocked out awareness of everything else? That's a form of hypnosis. Have you ever discovered yourself somewhere when driving your car, not remembering how you got there? That's road hypnosis. *Everyone can be hypnotized. Let me repeat; everyone can be – if they want it.* People often tell me "I can't be hypnotized." It's generally said as a challenge, and I'm supposed to reply something like this, "I'm an exceptional hypnotist I'll bet I can do it." My challenger is often disappointed when I immediately reply, "You're right!" *You cannot be hypnotized without desire.*

You or someone you know might have gone to a hypnotist who tried to work with you and didn't succeed. Have you ever taken a car to a mechanic to be fixed only to find the same problem when you got the car back? That didn't mean the car couldn't be fixed; it just meant that the car wasn't fixed by that mechanic at that time. If you have tried hypnosis and failed, all it means is that you weren't hypnotized by that hypnotist at that time. *Under the right conditions, anyone can experience hypnosis.*

■ **What about intelligence? Doesn't a very intelligent person "see through" hypnosis?** Actually, intelligent people are the best hypnotic subjects for several reasons:

1. Intelligent people are more interested in improving themselves and will do what it takes to perform at their best. Hypnosis helps you perform at your peak.

2. Intelligent people are more open minded and willing to learn about hypnosis. When people understand the truth about hypnosis, their concerns disappear.

3. Intelligent people are creative, a prerequisite for hypnosis. They are more successful in hypnosis than people with limited imaginations. *Actually, geniuses are often in a state of hypnosis when they are doing what makes them geniuses!*

■ **Why do I need hypnosis? Isn't behavior change mainly a matter of will power, determination, or persistent practice?** No one **needs** hypnosis, but if you want to change a behavior, overcome an unwanted habit or eliminate doubt and increase confidence, hypnosis is much faster and more effective than conscious will power, self-discipline, or positive thinking.

■ **Don't will power, self discipline and positive thinking work?** Sometimes, yes. Consistently, no. If they worked consistently, no one would be fat, people would-n't talk about giving up smoking or drinking or spending too much money or changing other habits; they would just do it. If will power and self-discipline worked consistently, people wouldn't procrastinate, wouldn't be working on income taxes the night of April 14. *If will power and discipline worked, there would be no slumps or yips, and golfers wouldn't fold under pressure.*

As a golfer, if you can eliminate yips quickly, why suffer with them? If you are in a slump, why stay there for a couple of years? *Hypnosis is a short cut, a support, and, it is effortless.*

■ **How does hypnosis work?** When you are in hypnosis, you are in a state of increased awareness and focus. You are highly open to and will carry out suggestions that are for your benefit. That's quite different from the misconception that a hypnotized person is "out of it" and gives up power to someone else. It is true that the person is in a "trance." *But the word trance to a hypnotist is simply a state of heightened awareness, concentration, and receptivity.*

A football fan so fixated on a Monday night game that he doesn't hear his wife talking to him is in a trance. A child watching Saturday morning cartoons is in a trance, and advertisers know that. Commercials are suggestions made to people in highly receptive states.

■

Hypnosis is the only way to get rid of a past history that holds you back. When you are in a totally relaxed and receptive hypnotic state, you can be desensitized to negative feelings such as fear or doubt. Behavior patterns such as missing short putts, or choking can be reprogrammed.

In hypnosis the judgmental conscious part of you is moved to the background. The subconscious comes to the fore. The hypnotist makes helpful suggestions for eliminating fear and doubt and for creating positive behavior change. You stop "beating yourself up." When your critical judgmental self is moved out of the way through hypnosis, your subconscious willingly accepts instructions that move you in positive directions. The old past history that keeps you from accomplishing your goals, living fully and joyfully is covered over.

This can be done with post-hypnotic suggestions. These suggestions are made while you are in the receptive hypnotic state and take effect later. For example, some post-hypnotic suggestions I have used with golfers are: "From now on, whenever you get ready to hit a ball, all concerns, doubts, and thoughts of previous poor shots disappear." "Whenever you get ready to hit, focus and concentration become intense," and "Whenever you step on the green, your muscles relax." This is a far cry from a stage show.

■ **What are the chances of my having a successful hypnotic experience?** That's up to you. If you say to yourself, "This is silly," or "I'm going to test or resist," then you won't get positive results. However, that's "cutting off your nose to spite your face." If you doubt or test, you won't be hypnotized and won't experience the benefits.

If you say to yourself, "I know I can't be hypnotized; I've tried, it doesn't work on me," you've already hypnotized yourself to believe it won't work. And it won't. This suggests that *all hypnosis is self-hypnosis.* This is true.

The hypnotist is your guide showing you how to get the results you want. If you doubt your own ability to go into the state, or decide for any reason not to follow the hypnotist's instructions, you won't get positive results. You can be successful only if you really want it. Some people can be deeply hypnotized almost immediately; for others it takes several tries. The key elements for success are a sincere desire for change and a belief that hypnosis will work for you. *If you are motivated and have an accepting attitude, you can be hypnotized and experience positive change.*

■ **How long do the hypnotic suggestions last?** Any suggestion can be canceled in a split second. Suggestions given by stage hypnotists for entertainment last minutes to hours. When it comes to hypnosis for desirable behavior change, it depends on a number of factors. One of the teachers with whom I studied hypnosis says that suggestions last about six months and then must be reinforced. That belief is passed on to her clients, and her suggestions last about six months. Another of my teachers gives examples of post-hypnotic suggestions lasting years. Suggestions made to eliminate fears or phobias can last a lifetime.

Chapter 13

Hypnosis in Sports:

The "Zone On Command"

Did you watch the pairs figure skating competition on television during the 1994 Winter Olympics? The Russian pair were the favorites to win but their practice was poor and the female partner and had been falling. When they were on the ice and warming up for the actual competition, the T.V. commentator said, "I don't see how this pair could possibly win the gold medal based on their performance in practice."

They skated flawlessly and won the gold medal. The coach was interviewed on camera after the performance and was asked "What happened since the practice – the performance was so much better?" The coach replied, "I hypnotized her."

Most viewers probably paid very little attention to this comment, but, as a hypnotist, I picked up on it immediately and was not surprised at all. I was not surprised because hypnosis is quite common in Russia and in many of the countries that used to comprise the Eastern Bloc – Rumania, Bulgaria, and what once was East Germany. As a matter of fact, hypnotists are part of the training contingent of their Olympic teams, which, by the way, win far more medals per capita than the United States.

The second reason I was not surprised is that hypnosis is incredibly effective in changing behavior quickly; in this case, falling and poor practice. The suggestions that were given to the skater probably involved confidence, relaxation, and forgetting or blocking out the memory of falling in practice. She was hypnotized to remember only her best performance. The subconscious mind took over and directed her body to reproduce an outstanding performance. With hypnosis, this is easy. In a totally "conscious" state, the mind naturally goes to the previous fear – that of falling. The muscles tighten and the body is set up to reproduce what is on the mind.

■

The first sports hypnosis research in the United States was done in 1943 by Professor Dorothy Yates at San Jose State College. She worked with six matched pairs of college boxers. One of each pair was trained in the traditional way; hypnosis was added to the training of the other. When the boxers fought each other, the hypnotized boxer won decisively in five cases out of six. The sixth match was a draw. As a result of this experiment, Dr. Yates trained the whole team, resulting in dramatic wins over stronger more experienced teams.

Boxer Ingmar Johannson trained with hypnosis before taking the world heavyweight championship from Floyd Patterson.

A team of eleven hypnotists accompanied the Russian athletes to the 1956 Olympics in Melbourne. Beginning in 1952, the Russians were the leading medal winners in four of the next seven Olympics, and number two in the other three.

A Swiss dentist, Dr. Raymond Abrezol, was a pioneer in the use of hypnotic mental training for athletes. In 1967, he was asked to work with the Swiss ski team. Before that time, the Swiss hadn't performed too well in the Olympics. In 1968, three of the four team members he worked with won Olympic medals. In the 1972 games, three more Swiss skiers won Olympic medals. A few years later, Dr. Richard Suinn, Professor of Psychology at Colorado State University, began working with the U.S. Olympic ski team. I am currently working with a cyclist, who is training for the 1996 Olympics.

Surprisingly, it is hard to find professional golfers who talk about using hypnosis. A number of my clients with high visibility have asked me not to tell anyone that they are using hypnosis. Yet, golf, the most mental of sports, lends itself so well to this advanced mental skill. Many golfers use variations of hypnosis, but are reluctant to call it by its name. It probably is for the same reason that most people shy away. They distrust or fear it, and it seems like "cheating." It seems too simple to work with a game as complex as golf. Grinding seems more legitimate.

■

I have found an unusually high level of acceptance by professionals on the Monterey Peninsula. Jim Langley, former tour player and current Head Professional at Cypress Point Club in Pebble Beach, used hypnosis as a touring pro more than thirty years ago.

Laird Small, Head Professional at Spyglass Hill in Pebble Beach, first used hypnosis to improve his own game fifteen years ago. He said that he became interested when he discovered that World Heavyweight Boxing Champion, Muhammed Ali, formerly Cassius Clay, used hypnosis as he was winning his titles. Small told me that, after his first session, he noticed an immediate improvement in his game. He used audiocassette tapes and noticed cumulative improvements. By the way, his consistent drive is longer than some of the top money winning touring pros.

Sally Dodge, 1994 LPGA Professional of the Year, and several other teaching professionals are my private clients – generally working with me before a tournament in which they feel extra pressure to perform well.

■

Golfers often experience "playing out of their minds," but they don't call it hypnosis. They say they are "playing in the zone." When players describe what it feels like to "play in the zone," they say they are in a state of heightened concentration. They are totally focused on each shot in a relaxed way, are aware only of the essentials, and are able to shut out all distractions, both physical and mental. Their confidence is high, they feel as though they can do no wrong. *The "zone" is a state of self-hypnosis. The "zone on command" is every athlete's dream.*

■

Unfortunately, you often hypnotize yourself to play poorly or to miss shots, You are not aware that you are hypnotizing yourself, but, any time you talk to yourself or give yourself instructions or suggestions when you are emotionally charged, light hypnosis can occur. Greg Norman bogeyed the second hole at the 1994 Masters. Afterwards, he said, "It was over after number two. I walked on that green thinking I could make four and walked off it with a six. The thought crossed my mind that it wasn't going to be my day." The thought, "It isn't going to be my day," directed his subconscious to give him what he asked for. It wasn't his day. He shot 77.

On the tee, in the rough, or when facing a crucial putt, you might think about a previous shot that you missed. This reminder in an emotional state increases the likelihood that you'll hit another poor shot. The second poor shot has a greater likelihood of producing the third, or even more until you play a bad round. This can easily produce another bad round. *To break potential slump behavior, a golfer must eliminate doubtful thoughts and cannot think about any previous poor shot.*

How do you get rid of doubt and other poor shot thoughts? A mental principal is that the mind can think only one thought at a time. Therefore, the only way to rid yourself of an unwanted thought is to immediately think about what you do want. You can do this consciously by constantly paying attention to what you say to yourself. You already learned the "Switch!" technique in Chapter 3.

Hypnosis makes it easier. Post-hypnotic suggestions can make you forget poor past shots. After playing in a state championship, a client called me and said, "My mind never wandered back to shots that I had missed. I just focused on the shot I was playing." When she came to me a week before the tournament, she told me that her coach kept telling her to focus on the present, but her mind kept jumping back to old missed shots. When that happens she said to herself, "I hope I don't do that again," not realizing that the subconscious doesn't understand "don't." After hypnosis, her mind stayed focused on the present.

Unwanted thoughts come into our minds uninvited. Usually, it is because there is a strong association of that thought or feeling with a place, a word, or an event. Let me give you an illustration. When you hear an "oldie, but goodie" on the radio, you remember a past event associated with that song. You might even have the same emotions you had then. The song that you and someone you love consider "your song" creates loving memories and feelings whenever you hear it. A song that was popular when an important relationship ended can recreate sadness every time you hear it.

Unfortunately, painful or negative experiences produce stronger and longer lasting memories than positive experiences. Neutral events have very little emotional impact on a person and are difficult to remember. When you play golf, if you have an uneventful round, you soon forget it. If you play a wonderful round, you remember it and talk about it for a while. If, however, you play a miserable round, especially during a tournament, that memory stays with you the longest.

You might have a strong emotional response to a shot. Maybe it's an embarrassing dribble off the first tee, the shot that lost the club championship, or, for a pro, the rushed approach shot that lands in the water on the eighteenth and costs $100,000. As you replay it and berate yourself for it, it can cause a permanent imprint on your subconscious. *The stronger your emotional response, the more likely it is you'll repeat the behavior.* Each repetition reinforces the same behavior.

If you watch tournament golf on T.V., you often see a player who can't putt that day. Usually, that player has had a negative emotional response to a missed putt, especially on the final day. The response doesn't have to be noticeable; generally, tour players keep their feelings in check. But if their self-talk sounds like, "You jerk, it's the third makable putt you've missed," "There goes another $50,000," or "Where are your guts when you need them?" they are creating the very condition they don't want – more missed putts.

The putter can become connected to negative emotions. When you hold the putter in your hand, the emotions of earlier missed putts are recreated. These emotions are transmitted to your muscles and you miss the next putt.

Remember, anxious thoughts create tension in the muscles. Just a tiny bit of tension leveraged with the putter pulls the putt off line. Another miss. More negative emotions. For the rest of the day, or much longer, easy putts are missed. Some pros change putters because they think they have bad luck with the one they've been using. Actually, it's not "luck." The old putter has many missed putts associated with it. The new putter is clean. It's a good tactic.

■

A good player can often self correct after disappointing holes, if he can "let go" emotionally. We saw this with Corey Pavin during the 1995 Ryder Cup. His team lost the Saturday morning match to Europe. Shortly before his spectacular chip on the eighteenth hole to win Saturday afternoon's match, he hit several poor shots. He was able to let go of those poor shots mentally and emotionally. When he let go, his muscles also let go of tension, and his easy, fluid, controlled, swing was back. For Pavin and the U.S., it meant a winning chip.

Had Betsy King mentally held onto her crucial mishit and berated herself for it at such an emotional time, she might have shot a bogey or worse on the first hole. Instead, she let the mishit go, recovered immediately, and was able to par the hole to go on and win the Shoprite Classic and her place in the Hall of Fame.

Many recreational players, and even some pros, tend to blow the entire hole, or several holes when they hit an unusually bad shot. Senior Tour player Isao Aioki was in the lead in the last round of the 1996 GTE Suncoast Classic. He hooked his tee shot into the water on the thirteenth hole. He took a drop, and his approach shot almost found the water again. Then, he hit wedges back and forth over the green, ending up with a 9 for the par 4 hole. He said he lost his patience. Each poor shot impacted the next. Had he been programmed to let go of previous poor shots, he probably would have kept his patience and concentration. Hypnosis to forget poor shots is easier and more reliable than efforting and willing to let go of poor shots. Had Aioki used self-hypnosis he could have controlled his thinking and kept his lead to win.

CHAPTER 14

WORKING WITH A HYPNOTIST

Basically, hypnosis is a quick, effective way to get into the subconscious mind and cross out, or paint over the negative emotions, erroneous beliefs and the bad habits that keep us from our full potential.

I use self-hypnosis for day to day desired behavior, confidence, concentration, putting, trusting my swing, my tennis game, and motivation for finishing this book. Sometimes, I am heavily invested in specific outcome. Doctors make it a rule not to treat family members because emotions get in the way of objectivity. As a certified hypnotherapist, when I find I am emotionally invested in an outcome, and my objectivity is clouded, I see a neutral colleague.

You can learn to hypnotize yourself from books. It takes time, practice and patience. (This is how I learned self-hypnosis twenty years before I studied formally and became certified.) You can learn the basics of self-hypnosis from Chapter 15 in this book. If you want quick results with much less effort, I recommend that you go to a reputable certified hypnotist, who specializes in athletic performance or, at the very least has worked with athletes. The hypnotist will guide you into hypnosis and make the appropriate suggestions for you.

Ask the hypnotist to teach you to hypnotize yourself. This can be done very easily. You'll want to be able to put yourself in the state when you play golf. ***When you learn to***

quickly put yourself into the state of heightened con-
sciousness and concentration you will be able to play in
the "zone on command. "

The right hypnotist is your guide to power performance. Choose your guide carefully. Just as each teaching professional has their own style and methods of teaching the swing, each hypnotist has a unique way of working with clients. It may take several attempts to find just the right person for you.

Though it's not essential, if your hypnotist plays your sport, so much the better. However, a good hypnotist can be taught to give you the right suggestions. When Laird Small wanted to use hypnosis to improve his game, he wrote out the suggestions he wanted implanted in his subconscious mind. He gave them to his hypnotist who then guided Small into hypnosis and gave him his own suggestions. When I work with athletes who play sports that I don't, I use a similar technique.

■

Generally, athletes who use hypnosis fall into three categories:

1. Those whose goal is to play their absolute best. They compete and want to develop their games to their maximum physical ability. Touring pros, serious amateurs, and Olympic hopefuls fall into this category.

2. Those who have a specific problem such as yips, or performance anxiety, and want that problem fixed.

3. People who enjoy the sport and would enjoy it more, if they played just a little bit better like the eighty-three-year-old woman who told me, "I love the game, but my thinking is limited, I'd like to regain my confidence."

Hypnosis works well for all types of motivated clients. When clients are hypnotized for a particular problem they generally experience a "positive spill over" effect to other parts of their lives.

■

When a client comes to work with me, I ask the following questions.

1. **"Why are you here? What are your goals? What do you want to accomplish by working with me?"** Typical answers: "If I know I'm playing with a much better player, I freeze up," and "I get too nervous and can't sleep before important tournaments." "My putting is off." "I want to win a major tournament." "I don't know what's wrong with my game; I'm playing just terrible." "I want to stop choking when it matters." "I just want to have more fun."

2. **"Tell me what happens when you are playing that doesn't work for you."** Typical comments might be, "I hit well on the practice range, but tense up and hit poorly when I actually play." "When I'm not playing well, I lose confidence and then try to fix my swing in the middle of a round." "I get so uptight when I putt that I leave most of them short or slam them way past the hole." "When I'm in the lead, my mind starts going wild."

3. **"Tell me about your successes."** My clients have made these comments: "I hit some fantastic drives down the middle." "I holed a 30 foot putt at a crucial time." "My partner and I won the member guest tournament." "I beat a scratch player." "I won major championships."

■

The next step is to educate the client as to what hypnosis is and what it can and can't accomplish. *Hypnosis cannot make you do what you are physically incapable of doing, but it can help you reach your full potential.* If your longest drive has been 210 yards, you won't drive like Laura Davies; however, some clients have been able to add about 15 yards to their tee shots. Hypnosis cannot create perfection or guarantee a great shot each time. *It can help you hit a great shot more often.* Remember, most tournaments are won by just one shot. *Hypnosis cannot guarantee a win, but it will increase the chances.*

When my clients are ready, I guide them into the hypnotic state with an induction. Induction is what the hypnotist does to create an open, receptive mind. Most hypnotists use a technique called progressive relaxation. It is a variation of the relaxation exercises in the Appendix. It can take quite a while to achieve the right level of hypnosis.

I generally use a more rapid method that has proven very effective. After some practice, my clients can reach the desired state of mental receptivity and concentration in just a few seconds. This is very handy for golfers because they can "hypnotize themselves" at will.

I create a customized set of suggestions based on our opening interview. Then I turn on my tape recorder, hypnotize them, make the suggestions and give them the audiocassette tape of the session. As the clients listen at home, the tape reinforces hypnosis, and drives the suggestions more deeply into the subconscious, assuring more lasting results.

If the goal – playing more confidently, getting rid of "yips" or being able to sleep before tournaments – is reached in one session, our work is done. Most clients, however, have more than one thing they want to work on, so I see them several times. They may come back months later to move to the next level.

I work with some clients by phone. During our first session, I condition them to accept my suggestions on tape or on the phone. One of my tennis playing clients rarely played on clay. She was practicing on clay courts just before a national tournament. She called and told me she was very uncomfortable on clay. I created a hypnotic tape for her and sent it overnight express. She was able to listen and be hypnotized before playing. She made it to the semi-finals.

Ultimately, the success of hypnosis depends on the clients. **If they have a strong desire to improve, and follow instructions, they can improve faster with hypnosis than with any other methods.**

Chapter 15
Self-Hypnosis:

Using the Four Keys

You have enough information on the **Four Keys** to know that they will improve your game. You also know enough about hypnosis to understand how powerful a tool it can be. Combining the two will give you amazing performance breakthroughs and help you play in the **"zone on command."**

This chapter gives you the basics of self-hypnosis. Just as it takes time and practice to get a good swing, it takes time and practice to get good results from self-hypnosis. So be patient with yourself and practice.

Set aside time regularly to devote to self-hypnosis. You must choose a time and place where you will be undisturbed and can concentrate.

STEP 1.
Relax. (Learn how to do self-induction.)
If you have practiced the relaxation exercises in Appendix A, you know what relaxed muscles feel like. You won't use this particular relaxation exercise to hypnotize yourself. Instead, use the hypnotic induction in Appendix J. A hypnotic induction is designed to put you into the "trance" your subconscious mind needs to accept your suggestions. To reach this state will take some time and practice at first, but as you continue to practice, it will take

less and less time. People skilled at self-hypnosis can put themselves into a trance in a matter of seconds. This will be very handy for you on the golf course.

STEP 2.

Decide on the specific changes or improvements you want to make in your golf game. Write out scripts.

Include "Great Shot Thoughts" in Your Script. When you go to a hypnotist, you are given affirming suggestions for the conditions you want. Each time you hypnotize yourself, decide on the suggestions you want before you begin.

Examples of simple suggestions I make for some of my golfing clients include: "You are confident in your ability to hit the ball well," or "All thoughts of previous poor shots disappear." "When you are ready to hit the ball, you are undisturbed by distractions." One suggestion I created for Hollis Stacy is, "Whenever, you step on the green, you relax and focus." After she played her first post-hypnosis tournament, she said, "I couldn't have been more focused." What suggestions will help you?

Include Visualization in Your Script. What you see is what you get. Most good teaching professionals tell their students to do some sort of visualization before hitting the ball. Unfortunately, most golfers have already spent a lot of time anxiously visualizing the ball in the bunker or water hazard. The verbal instructions given by the pro most often don't override the old negative visualizations.

A talented young junior told me that she learned all about visualization and explained to me exactly how she was taught to do it. Then, she added, "But when I get ready to hit, I'm not sure it's going to work." Visualization doesn't work for her because her doubt thoughts create exactly what she doesn't want. *Hypnosis eliminates doubt thoughts.* Visualizations done in the conscious state don't have nearly the power that hypnotic suggestions have.

When you write your scripts, make sure they include vivid visual and kinesthetic images.

The following is a complete script for chipping I created for a golfer with input from her teaching pro. This player had already been through my hypnotic conditioning in which I suggest that, "In the future, whenever I hypnotize you in person, on the phone, or on tape, you go quickly and deeply into the hypnotic state that will help you to do the work you want for your benefit."

As you learn self-hypnosis, begin with induction in Appendix J. When you are good at putting yourself into a "trance," you can shorten the induction to the one below.

Take a deep breath and, as you exhale, allow your eyes to close. Another breath and, as you exhale slowly, let all surface tension melt from your body. Remember the feelings you had when I hypnotized you? Recreate those feelings. I will guide you. It is your desire to go into a deep comfortable state of hypnosis where your subconscious mind will accept the suggestions you want and I give you to improve your golf game. Go quickly and deeply. With each gentle breath you exhale, you go deeper and deeper into the wonderful, comfortable, desirable state of hypnosis.

Feeling the total relaxation of your head, when you are ready, test your eyes to see that they are so relaxed, they don't want to, nor can they, open. Now, take that same level of relaxation and send it through the rest of your body. The relaxation is so complete that your arms feel they don't have the power to move. When you have reached that level of relaxation, test your left arm to see that it does not want to, nor can it, move. Now, your left arm returns to normal; test it to see that it has a complete range of motion.

You want to go as deeply as you can. Imagine yourself at the top of a staircase, with ten steps. Is it carpeted, wooden, marble, curved, or straight? See it vividly. With each number I say, take one step down, with each step down, allow yourself to go deeper and deeper into this wonderful, comfortable, hypnotic state. 10, 9, deeper and deeper, 8, 7, feeling so good, so comfortable 6, so beautifully relaxed, 5, 4, going deeper, 3, you are almost where you want to be, 2, 1. You are now at the level at which you want to accept suggestions to improve your golf game.

Transport yourself mentally to the fairway, just short of the green. Imagine yourself there. Notice what you are wearing, where you are standing. The right club for the conditions is in your hand. See the flag at the cup gently fluttering. Now, imagine yourself setting up, going through your preshot routine. Watch yourself as you execute the perfect chip. See the ball land on the green and roll toward and into the hole. Perfect. Do that again. See yourself as though you were watching yourself on T.V. See the perfect chip. Great shot.

Now, put yourself inside your body so you can experience all the sensations. Once more transport yourself to the fairway. This time, you feel the grass under your feet, your club in your hand, the breeze on your face. You are on the fairway. Feel yourself setting up, how your body feels when it is in perfect position. Feel yourself, going through your preshot routine. Your breathing is slow and easy and, when you are ready, be aware of the sensations in your body as you take your backswing and then hit the ball. Feel your follow-through, and now watch the ball roll toward the hole. Another great shot.

You can chip this way because you have had a lesson from a professional on chipping and pitching. You know the correct steps to take to create your desired results. Let's recreate that now.

Imagine yourself with your pro, listening to and following instructions. See the dimpled white ball. Line yourself up. See and feel yourself placing your feet in the proper position, parallel to the target or slightly open, closer together than for other shots. Feel the extra bend at the waist as your hands are down near the bottom of the grip. Your knees are comfortably bent, weight slightly toward the left. See the ball positioned toward your right foot. Feel your left arm and club create a straight line, and notice your hands are slightly in front of the ball. Check that the face of the clubhead is square to the target.

When you are ready, take a focusng breath and visualize the flight of the ball, feel yourself take a short backswing to just the right height, now rock your shoulders to the left, allowing the arms to swing, keeping the left wrist firm as the club head makes contact. Hear the sound as the club makes contact with the ball and feel the follow through, aware that your left wrist is still firm. Feel those sensations in your body. Now, hear the voice of your pro exclaim 'Nice shot' as your ball rolls toward the hole.

Imagine yourself hitting another chip shot feeling and seeing yourself do that. Do it again and again. Now practice that shot several times, noticing that every time you practice, it becomes smoother and easier. Now, you have finished practice for the day. You feel that you have hit well and made real progress.

When you play a round on the golf course, you now feel confident that you chip well. Imagine yourself in a game. See yourself on the fairway, just short of the green. See yourself there; notice what you are wearing, where you are standing. You have your club in your hand. See the flag at the cup gently fluttering. Now, imagine yourself setting up, going through your preshot routine. Feel all the sensations in your body. Imagine yourself as you execute the perfect chip. See the ball land on the green and roll toward and into the hole. Perfect. Feel the excitement of having hit just the shot you wanted.

I am going to bring you back to here and now by counting backwards from 5 to 1. When I reach 1, your eyes will open, you will feel more refreshed than you have felt in a long time. 5. Slowly easily, comfortably coming back to here and now. 4. Energetic, motivated, enthusiastic about your game. 3. Totally confident that you have the skills to make good shots for your level of play. 2. Knowing that listening to your tapes regularly improves your game. 1. Alert aware, opening your eyes, feeling refreshed and wonderful.

You probably noticed the **Four Key** elements in this script: first the relaxation, then all positive words, and a lot of visualization.

If you are preparing for an important tournament, create the perfect round in all it's detail (except for the time between shots), and record it. You can play the round over and over in hypnosis, which can be more effective than playing a practice round.

Create a personalized script for each part of your game. Read the script into a tape recorder. Then you can *practice in bed.*

It is not necessary to formally write out a long script every time you hypnotize yourself. You can hypnotize yourself and make short affirming great shot statements, such as, "I am relaxed and play with confidence," "I trust my swing and putting stroke," or "My putt is smooth and on line." When you are able to hypnotize yourself very quickly, you can call up the **"zone on command."**

■

Most of us put ourselves into hypnotic states several times a day. It happens when we daydream, drive, watch a movie, sit at our computers, or concentrate on a hobby, or are in the "zone." We are so totally focused we are unaware of anything else. In this state we do our best work and best play.

Now that you know the steps for self-hypnosis, you can deliberately create this state. You will have control of your thoughts, your behavior, and be able to play "out of your mind." As you will learn in the next chapter, the **Four Keys** and hypnosis can enhance every area of your life.

PART V

APPLYING THE FOUR KEYS TO YOUR LIFE

*If you want greater success in your professional life or to change unwanted habits – modify the **Four Keys**. This part will tell you how! Adapt the Keys to any area of your life.*

CHAPTER 16
THE KEYS TO A SUCCESSFUL LIFE

If you read books on success, or talk to successful people, they will all tell you that:

1. If you want to outperform the field, you must be motivated and have a real desire to excel.

2. You must have the technical skills or know how.

3. You must manage your mind and believe in your ability to produce results.

4. You must be willing to do what it takes to achieve your goals.

The basic elements of peak performance are the same, whether you want to be a great golfer or super salesperson.

I can't give you the desire or motivation. I can't give you the technical skills, and I can't give you the determination and persistence necessary to succeed. *I can teach you how to manage your mind for success.*

I systematized and simplified the elements of mental management and developed **Four Keys** to breakthrough performance. They can be adapted to enhance performance in any area. This book is *Mental Management for Great Golf;* it could also be Mental Management for Terrific Tennis, Mental Management for Super Sales, Mental Management for Excellence in Exams, Mental Management for Creative Communication, Mental Management for Building Your Business. Mental Management for Confidence and Self Esteem. We could go on and on.

Take the principles you have learned for improving your golf game, modify and use them, wherever and whenever you want to excel.

■

I heard an interview with Mark Victor Hanson and Jack Canfield, authors of the *Chicken Soup* books. Their books had sold over five million copies in less than two years, and more sequels are in the making. The authors described the process of writing best sellers. Their process involved three of the **Four Keys.** The only thing not mentioned in the interview was formal relaxation, but I have a feeling that when they visualized and practiced in bed, they were in a relaxed state.

I'm going to show you how the **Four Keys** can work in several areas of life. You can practice them in the fully conscious state or in the hypnotic state. The hypnotic state has more power. *As in sports, when you use hypnosis in other areas of your life, you will get faster results.*

Applying the Keys in Sales.
Many salespeople have a problem with cold calls. If that's your problem, you might tell yourself things like, "I hate to cold call," "People don't want to talk to me." "Oh, no, it's time to make calls again," and so on. Each of these comments reinforces your call reluctance. *Changing your self-talk changes your attitude and changes your behavior.* Try these more constructive comments: "Here is my opportunity to meet potential clients," "People who want what I have to sell will never find me if I don't cold call." "One of every ten or twenty (whatever your number), people I call is a yes. I can hardly wait to get my yes."

If you are a reluctant cold caller, create visualizations of, and imagine yourself on the phone with a list of prospects, calling one after another until the calls are complete.

It is very helpful to have "scripts," not to read stiffly into the phone, but to have a list of appropriate sales oriented questions to ask the prospect, answers to questions and objections, and points you want to make. This script can be rehearsed over and over (practiced in bed), until you reach a comfort level that makes cold calling simple.

Just as people can be hypnotized to overcome other fears and phobias, they can be hypnotized to overcome call reluctance.

Using the Keys and Hypnosis to Overcome the Fear of Public Speaking.

The most common fear in the United States is the fear of speaking in front of a group. This fear is similar to first tee jitters, but more serious. Both involve performance anxiety. Practicing the **Four Keys** is a remedy for both, however, both respond more quickly to hypnosis.

The more you talk about a problem, the more the subconscious mind focuses on it. My *first recommendation for people who have performance anxiety is to stop talking about the problem and anticipate, talk, and think about the solution.* The solution involves the ability to perform with the right amount of positive arousal rather than incapacitating fear.

Since we become what we think, talk about, and imagine, let's think, talk about, and imagine easy, comfortable, confident, high level performance. Jack Nicklaus made mental movies of the shots he wanted. Using the same principle, if you have a fear of public speaking, make a mental movie of the perfect presentation. I know that when you begin to imagine the perfect presentation or say to yourself, "I am comfortable getting up in front of a group," you'll probably consider it a lie. But the more often lies are repeated, the truer they seem. Eventually, the myth becomes a reality.

Method acting or "pretending" works especially well with this fear. If you were a comfortable public speaker, how would you, look, feel, act? Recall a riveting presentation given by someone else. Pretend you are this person. Visualize this vividly. Practice it in bed.

One of my clients, a prominent attorney and senior partner with the world's largest law firm, had a problem speaking in front of groups. Using "will power" to get over it was not effective, and limiting her practice to corporate law too restrictive. One session of hypnosis accomplished what years of struggle and will power hadn't.

Relax and Let Go. The Best Way to Take Exams.

If you are a student, or have a student in your family, the techniques for superlearning and recall for exams are the same basic techniques used for athletic achievement. The student is advised first to study and develop the skill. If studying is done in a relaxed focused state, the subconscious will store the material permanently on the brain cells. When it is time to take an exam, relaxation will cause the subconscious to give back the material easily.

When students take high stakes exams, such as college entrance or bar exams, their extreme level of anxiety actually keeps the subconscious from finding the answer. Have you ever left an exam room and then have the right answers just pop into your head? Once the exam is over, test anxiety disappears. The subconscious then remembers where it put the answers. Relaxing before the exam allows the subconscious to remember the material at the right time.

Using the Four Keys in Your Personal Life.

Almost any behavior can be influenced or changed through the conscious application of the **Four Keys**, or by using hypnosis. These methods have been used for weight control, overcoming procrastination, disorganization, to stop smoking, to learn a new skill, change a career, develop new friendships, enhance interpersonal communication, to become a better parent, and much more.

How would you like to use these techniques to enhance your life? Once you have decided what you want to change or accomplish, set specific goals – this helps create motivation and desire. Learn to relax physically, which leads to mental relaxation, clarity, focus, and concentration. The next step is to *think only great performance or desired behavior thoughts.* Eliminate all negative self-talk. For example, I changed my golf self-talk from, "I'm a lousy player" to "I'm a developing golfer." Then, in a state of relaxation, visualize yourself and your life as you would like it to be. This gives the subconscious mind the blueprint from which to build your best self. Practice in bed and act as if it were all true. Before long, it will be!

You now have several examples of how the **Four Keys** can be modified and adapted to enhance your performance and bring you success in any area. With this knowledge you have the most powerful tool for changing behavior and controlling your life – Mental Management.

A. PROGRESSIVE RELAXATION

Duration: About 20 minutes

This exercise is a combination and simplification of Jacobson's muscle relaxation, Johannes Schultz's autogenic training, and several other well known relaxation techniques. Read the directions for this relaxation. You will notice a pattern. Then you can put yourself through the exercise by recalling the steps. If you leave a few out, it won't matter. We're just concerned about the end result – a relaxed body and mind. If someone is willing to read the directions to you slowly, you won't have to think about steps, but merely follow directions.

Try slowly reading the instructions into a tape recorder. and play the tape daily for practice until muscle relaxation becomes second nature. (For best results, you could order my audiocassette relaxation tape which is wonderful for general relaxation and insomnia.)

Find a comfortable place where you can stretch out and be undisturbed for about 20 minutes. A bed is good, as is a pad on the floor, or just a comfortable carpet. If you are wearing glasses, take them off. Take off your shoes, too. Loosen any tight belts, ties, pinching earrings.

You are going to tense and relax each muscle group in turn. The instructions tell you to hold each change for 10 to 15 seconds. For those who are intent upon being exact, this is not an exercise in timing, it is an exercise in becoming familiar with the difference in feelings between tension and relaxation. Actually, you want to become especially familiar with relaxation – you are generally tense enough. When you tense, try to create so much tension that your muscles quiver. When you relax, imagine the tension just flowing out of your body. There will be times when parts of your body feel so good that you'll want to stop and enjoy the feeling for more than 15 seconds. That's fine. Do not feel compelled to rush ahead to the next part.

Close your eyes. We'll start with your toes. Curl your toes and create tension. Curl as hard as you can and focus on the feeling. Hold for about 10 seconds. Now let go, wiggle your toes into relaxation. Point your toes upward and create tension in your feet, feeling the pulling in your heels. Hold for about 10 to 15 seconds and release. For 10 to 15 seconds focus on the feelings in your feet. Now, as hard as you can, tense the muscles of your lower legs. Hold for 10 or more seconds. Let go and become sensitive to the feelings in your lower legs and feet. Next, you'll tense your thigh muscles, and again hold for 10 to 15 seconds. Let go. Each time you tense a set of muscles and let them go, focus on the sensations for 10 seconds or more. Repeat this tension and relaxation with your entire leg.

It's time to move upward. Tense and squeeze your buttocks, holding the tension for 10 to 15 seconds then letting go. Remaining flat on your surface, crunch your abdominal muscles. Pull in, tighter, tighter. Release. Now tense the large muscles of your back. Hold, and relax. Shrug your shoulders up to your ears. A 10 to 15 second hold. Let go, relax. Create tension in your arms now. Can you do this without tensing your hands? Concentrate on creating the tension only in your arms. Let go of the tension. Now make as tight a fist as you can. Hold. Are you aware of the rest of your body tensing as you make the fist? After some practice, it will be easier to tense only one part of the body at a time. Let go.

Now we'll tense and relax the muscles of your face and head. Start with your jaw. Tense. Relax. Tense your scalp by furrowing your brow and squeezing your eyes shut as tightly as you can. Notice and hold on to the tension for about 10 seconds. Then, let go and allow the muscles to relax. Become aware of your eyelids gently covering your eyes. Pretend there is a relaxation mask on your face. Your skin is smooth. Compare the feelings. To complete the muscle tension/relaxation cycle, tense your entire body. Hold, and let go. As your body relaxes, focus on your breathing and breathe relaxation into your entire body.

Next, focus your attention on the feelings in your limbs. Are your arms and legs heavy? Light and tingly? Are your limbs warm, cool? Become aware of the sensations. Starting with your arms, imagine that they are heavy. Try to create a feeling of heaviness in them. Beginning with your dominant arm, focus on the sensations. Just repeat over and over to yourself, "My arm feels heavy, my arm feels heavy." It might help to imagine that you have a heavy object in your hand, or that your arm is covered with a heavy blanket. When you have created a feeling of heaviness in one arm, focus your attention on the other arm and make it feel as heavy as you can without effort; just give your arms verbal directions to feel heavy. Repeat this exercise with your legs. First one leg, making it heavy, heavy, heavy, breathing heaviness into it. Then the other leg. Become aware of the heaviness in your legs. Now notice your entire body sinking into the surface you are lying on. So relaxed, you feel immobile. Revel in this relaxed feeling and stay here as long as you like.

When you are ready to resume your normal activities, breathe energy into your body and slowly begin moving your limbs in smooth relaxed motions. Carry this relaxation with you into your daily life.

This exercise teaches you to relax your body. You know that when your muscles are relaxed, you cannot have anxious stressful thoughts. Learning to relax the body is a skill that can bring more stillness and peace to every aspect of your life.

■

The next relaxation technique moves in the opposite direction. We begin by relaxing the mind and, as a result create relaxation in the body.

B. A RELAXING PLACE

Duration: About 5 to 10 minutes
This exercise focuses on relaxing your mind, which then will produce relaxed muscles. You probably already do a variation of this exercise, and sometimes feel guilty about it because "daydreaming" isn't generally considered productive. Well, it is. Short periods of focused daydreaming are refreshing, rejuvenating, and relaxing. It is physically and mentally healthy.

You can do this relaxing exercise seated or lying down. Close your eyes. Take a slow, deep, relaxing breath. For a minute or two, count as you slowly breathe, feeling each breath as it you breathe in through your nose and out through your mouth. Then transport yourself mentally to a time and place in which you were completely relaxed and carefree. You might want to go back to a wonderful childhood experience – perhaps camping at the side of a deep blue lake, surrounded by spectacular trees, maybe fishing in a cool mountain stream, or walking on the beach on a warm summer day. Maybe your carefree place was a corner in your bedroom where you felt safe and secure on dreary winter days. Create that scene in your mind.

If you prefer, you can relive a wonderful experience you had as an adult. You can mentally transport yourself back to a magnificent cruise ship sailing on the vast sea, or playing golf at Pebble Beach. (Recreate only the spectacular setting and joyful feelings and not the frustration of the balls in the surf.)

When you have recalled that happy relaxing scene, relive it. Imagine yourself there again. Imagine your surroundings in brilliant color, relive that past in as much detail as you can. Hear the sounds around you, smell the scents, feel the physical feelings as you recall and relive that experience.

If you haven't had these kinds of experiences yet, fantasize a marvelous future scene in your mind. Imagine yourself in any totally wonderful, completely relaxing place. Create it as you would have it occur. Live it in all it's detail, color, sounds, scents, feelings. Be there in your imagination. And, as your mind wraps around this imagined experience, the muscles in your body will completely relax. When you feel marvelous and become aware of a smile on your face, you can open your eyes, keeping the relaxation with you.

You can use this type of exercise to fall asleep at night or to take a few minutes of vacation from the stress and concerns of the day.

C. DEEP BREATHING
Duration: About 1 to 2 minutes
Its easiest to learn deep breathing with your eyes closed. Closed eyes shut out distractions and help you focus on the sensations in your body. To do the easy breathing that will eliminate the tension in your muscles, the breath must be slow and deep, as though you were breathing into your stomach. As you inhale gently through your nose, imagine that air is filling your stomach. Yes, your stomach, not your lungs. Put your hands on your abdomen. If you are inhaling relaxing breaths, your abdomen, not your chest

will rise. When you exhale slowly through your mouth, your abdomen flattens. Say to yourself, "re" as you inhale, and "lax," as you exhale. As you learn to deep breathe, take just a few breaths each time you practice – too much at once can cause dizziness or discomfort. With gradual practice, deep breathing becomes more comfortable and natural for you. Before long, with regular practice, you will be able to totally let go of all tension in your muscles with one breath. This is your goal as you move toward the next step.

D. PRESHOT BREATHING

Duration: 5 to 10 seconds

If you have been practicing the relaxation exercises and the one to two minute deep breathing, whenever you notice physical tension or mental distraction, you should be able to take one deep cleansing breath and relax on the exhalation. If you work in a deep breath and exhale just prior to your backswing, your body relaxes, your mind relaxes, and your swing will be freer, truer and more consistent. The deep breath is especially helpful as you stand over your putt, ready to stroke. The breath should be the last part of the preshot routine, because it helps you let go of the distracting instructions you probably have given yourself.

When you have mastered these techniques, you will be able to relax your muscles and clear your mind at will. That's what you want. When your muscles are relaxed, you cannot have anxious shot-ruining thoughts. When your mind is clear, and your muscles relaxed, focus and concentration are a natural state.

E. LEARNING TO VISUALIZE

Read each description through first, then follow the instructions.

1. Close your eyes, take a deep breath, relax. Now with your eyes closed, how many windows are in your living room? kitchen? bedroom, or office? How did you count them? To count, you must have created an image of the room in your mind. That's visualization.

2. Think back to this morning when you or your partner left the house. What did he/she have on when you said good-bye to each other? (If you live alone, try something else.)

3. In your mind, trace the route you take between your home and work, or the shopping center, or your home and the golf course.

4. With your eyes closed, take a deep breath, and imagine yourself completely alone in a spectacular and private setting. You might be on a warm tropical beach, perhaps in a suite in a luxury hotel. Now imagine that an absolutely gorgeous person of the opposite sex joins you in that private place. Since we're creating a fantasy here, take several minutes to play that fantasy out in all it's detail and notice your physical sensations. What is happening to your body? All you did was think, and your body reflected your thoughts.

5. Here's one you might recognize. You are waiting for someone you care about to come home. It's a dark and rainy night and the person is late. Recreate the feelings you had when, as it got later and later, your thoughts turned to an accident. Remember that sick-to-your stomach feeling? It was created by the stories you told yourself. Now feel the anxiety, tension, doubt. Now imagine hitting a golf ball with those feelings. You'd probably rather go back to the last fantasy. O.K., go ahead. Now, imagine hitting a golf ball with the pleasant feelings!

6. Transport yourself mentally to your favorite golf course and describe in detail what you see as you get ready to play. What are you wearing? See the cart in your minds eye. What color is it? Or do you walk? What do you see and hear as you go to the first green? From the tee box, look out over the green and toward the flag. Experience the green of the grass, imagine the sky blue. Imagine yourself looking at and holding the ball. Feel the weight of the ball in your hands and the dimples on the surface. Imagine yourself taking a club out of the bag. What color is the bag? Which club are you pulling out? Can you feel the weight of the club, the texture of the grip? All of this is visualization. Keep practicing, and you'll soon be able to visualize the flight or roll of the ball.

GENERIC VISUALIZATION SCRIPTS

These generic scripts are for the recreational player who wants to play more relaxed and confident and have more fun. The wording is appropriate for recording and then playing your own recording back, or for having someone else read the scripts to you. If you choose not to record these scripts, but rather read and then think them to yourself, substitute the word "I" for the word "you." For serious competitors, I write more detailed scripts customized to their specific needs. Instead of recording scripts yourself you can order a set of my visualization tapes. Ordering information is in the back of the book.

F. PREPARING TO PLAY

Duration: About 10 minutes

If you practice this visualization once a day for a few weeks, or several times a day for a week or so, preparation will become a conditioned response. There is no hard and fast rule about how long it will take. Each individual is different. Just "practice in bed" until you become aware that it is working. Reinforce periodically.

Sit or lie down in a comfortable place where you will be undisturbed for about 10 minutes. Close your eyes and focus on your breathing as you inhale relaxation and exhale tension and stress. Put yourself in a state of physical and mental relaxation using your favorite method, either the muscle relaxation or mental relaxation technique. If you have already become adept at relaxation, a two minute breathing exercise might be enough.

When you are totally relaxed, imagine yourself getting ready to play a round of golf. You want to be calm, focused, and have relaxed confidence as you play. Visualize yourself getting into your car to drive to the golf course. First you open the door; then, get in and sit in the driver's seat and roll down the window. You fasten your seat belt. Now, just sit for a moment, breathing deeply and letting go of the cares and concerns of the day. Imagine yourself doing that now, inhaling deeply, feeling relaxation flow into your body. As you exhale, imagine your cares and concerns flowing out the open window. Only the positive confident thoughts remain in your mind. Should any doubt or negative thought surface, send it out the window on your next exhalation and invite a confident thought in with your next breath.

Now imagine yourself driving to the golf course relaxed and eager to play. Imagine a smile on your face as you anticipate a good round with congenial people in beautiful surroundings. The closer you get to the golf course, the better you feel. Feel your confidence build up. Know that you have a good repertoire of shots; that you have the ability to hit good shots for your level of play. Know that whatever happens on the course, you'll be able to handle it in the most appropriate way. Enjoy these thoughts and feelings for a while and, when you are ready, open your eyes.

G. CONFIDENCE

In a state of relaxation, practice the following visualization often. Remember to change the wording to "I" if you repeat it to yourself rather than record and listen to it.

You have the ability to play an excellent game of golf. You have confidence in your golf game. You know the fundamentals, you know course management, and your mechanics are excellent. You have hit outstanding shots with your woods, your long irons, your short irons. You have made outstanding putts. You have confidence that your muscles know how to hit excellent shots.

Your game is dependent on you, not on other people. You play extremely well for your level of play and experience. You and only you are in charge of and have influence on your game. You have confidence that you can play extremely well, because you have done it in the past. Know that your muscles remember how to play well. Your muscles remember how to hit each shot well. With relaxation, you allow your muscles to freely do what they know how to do.

You can create relaxed confidence to keep with you whenever you are on the golf course, regardless of conditions, who you are playing with, or who is watching. You are relaxed and confident, regardless of the stakes. You have relaxed confidence any time you are on the golf course. Recreate that feeling now. Be aware of the smile on your face, your confident walk, your shoulders back, head straight. Yes, you are relaxed and confident.

Now, imagine yourself getting ready to play. Take a deep breath, release all tension. You relax more and more. Now, imagine yourself walking toward the first tee. As you approach the tee, you breathe calmly, deliberately. As you breathe, you breathe out all tension, doubts, or anxieties about your performance. You know you play well. You know you have the skills. Imagine yourself now saying to yourself, "I play well. I have excellent skills, as I breathe deeply, all tension leaves, and relaxed confidence sets in." Breathe relaxed confidence. You associate the golf course with relaxed confidence, regardless of conditions, who you are playing with, who is watching, and regardless of the stakes. You always play with relaxed confidence; you know you have the skills and ability so allow your body to do what it knows how to do – breathe relaxed confidence. That is the signal to let go of any tension, doubts or anxieties about your performance.

You feel relaxed confidence. Now tee off in your imagination. Get lined up – ready – visualize your target and the trajectory of the ball. Feel the energy of your swing. Hear the sound of the club hitting the ball. Great shot! Feel the feeling of exhilaration as you watch the ball soar and hit your intended target area. You feel so good, you feel so confident, you feel so relaxed about your game and your ability You play the rest of the hole and the rest of the match with the same relaxed confidence.

Should the slightest feeling of doubt surface, at any time during play, you immediately take a deep breath, repeat "relaxed confidence" and feel your muscles relax and your mind clear. Should you occasionally hit a poor shot, recognize that this is temporary, that the rest of your shots will be excellent. You block out all thoughts of an occasional poor shot and focus only on your abilities and skills.

Now, mentally transport yourself to the last hole for today. Feel the exhilarated feeling that you have played well. You have been relaxed and confident throughout the match, no matter what the conditions. Feel the feeling of pride that you have played extremely well; you are pleased with your score. In your mind's eye, play out the last hole.

Sense the satisfaction you feel as your last putt rolls down the line. Hear the ball hit the bottom of the cup. You are an excellent golfer and you play with relaxed confidence at all times.

When you are ready, open your eyes, feel calm, confident, and relaxed.

H. TEE SHOTS

In a state of relaxation, mentally transport yourself to the first tee. Visualize your surroundings in detail: the fairway, the bright green grass, the blue sky, your playing companions. Imagine yourself getting ready to tee off, feeling relaxed and confident. Create those feelings in yourself now. Hear yourself say to yourself, "I feel relaxed and confident." Be aware that your breathing is slow and deep – very comfortable. Your thoughts are great shot thoughts. You know you are going to hit well. Before it is your turn to tee off, think about how you are going to play this hole. Pick a target, a specific small target, for your shot. What club are you going to use? Think only of a great shot. Imagine your ball soaring through the air; feel the exhilaration as you visualize it rising, making it's way to the target.

It's your turn to tee off. Feel the tee take hold in the ground as you position the tee and ball. Now, take a moment to imagine yourself and feel yourself go through your entire preshot routine. Line up, focus and concentrate on the target. Take a relaxing preshot breath, address the ball, and as you take the backswing, trust your subconscious to direct your muscles to make all the right moves. Feel the swing, hear the crack of the clubhead hitting through the ball, feel the flow of the followthrough and visualize the ball taking the right flight to the target. It lands. You feel wonderful as you hear your partner exclaim, "great shot."

Practice the shot off the first tee in your mind several times. The more you practice mentally, the better you will play.

Now, allow yourself to drift back to here and now. When you are ready, open your eyes, feeling refreshed, relaxed, alert, aware, motivated, and totally confident in your ability to hit great tee shots.

I. PUTTING

Put yourself in a comfortable, relaxed state, either with progressive relaxation or a breathing technique.

When you are ready, transport yourself mentally to the putting green. Visualize the short clipped grass, notice the slightly longer fringe. See the flagstick marking the cup. What color is the flag on your imagined flagstick? Notice where your ball has landed on the green. How far is it from the cup? Imagine yourself reading the greens and thinking about what you need to do to sink the putt. Whenever you look at the cup or the ball, always visualize that ball finding its target, the hole.

It's your turn to putt. Visualize yourself determining speed, distance and break, imagining the line the ball will follow on its way to the hole. Line up. In your mind, go through your complete preshot routine, feeling it in your muscles. You feel relaxed and confident standing over the putt. You know you have holed many putts in the past. Imagine yourself taking a few seconds to visualize the putt rolling down the line and falling into the cup. Imagine the sound as the ball hits the bottom. Take an easy relaxing breath. Now imagine yourself smoothly take the putter back and stroke. A perfect stroke, good followthrough, now, in your imagination, watch the ball follow its intended path to the cup. It drops. You feel very pleased, but actually expected the great shot. Hear your partner admire the putt.

You want to practice this same routine with putts of different lengths. When you are finished practicing in your mind, and when you are ready to open your eyes, open them feeling relaxed, motivated and confident of being a great putter.

J. HYPNOTIC INDUCTION

When you decide to hypnotize yourself, read this induction into a tape recorder at a slow, relaxing tempo. Then add the suggestions that you want embedded in your subconscious mind.

Sit or lie down in a relaxed and comfortable position, arms and legs uncrossed, any tight clothing loosened. Take a slow, deep, breath and, as you exhale, allow your eyes to close. Focus your attention on your breathing. Become aware of and feel the air entering your nostrils. With each exhalation, breathe out tension and stress. It is your desire to put yourself into a wonderful, easy, relaxing state of hypnosis. Follow my instructions and this will happen for you.

Focus your attention on your scalp and notice it relax. As a warm wave of relaxation begins at the top of your head and slowly moves downward, feel the relaxation ease the furrows in your brow. Your forehead feels smooth. All the little muscles around your eyes relax. Your eyes feel so heavy, almost as though they were comfortably glued together. Feel the wave of relaxation move down your face, relaxing your jaw. You might feel more comfortable letting your lips part slightly. Now, relaxation circles your neck and moves down into your shoulders. All the tension you might have had in your shoulders lets go. It feels as though the weight of the world has been lifted from your shoulders.

It feels easier to breathe, as your chest muscles relax. Your breath is slower and deeper. Now, feel the wave of relaxation move into your upper back and the muscles around your vertebrae let go. Relaxation moves down your back and around into your stomach and pelvis. Breathing deeply and slowly, you become more aware of the surface supporting your body. Feel your body sinking into that surface as you breathe in more relaxation.

Now, feel your leg muscles let go; first your thighs and then your shins and calves. The wave of relaxation circles your ankles and moves into your feet. Allow the relaxation to push whatever tension you might have had in your lower body out your toes. You might even feel some tingling in your toes. Focus your attention on your arms. Notice that your biceps and triceps let go, and your arms become loose, limp, and relaxed. Do you feel a light, fluid sensation in your hands? They are so relaxed. Take a few minutes to revel in this feeling of relaxation and peace. Should there be any noise or distractions while you are hypnotized, they will not bother you; they will only serve to send you deeper into this desirable state. The only sound that you attend to is the sound of my voice as I give you suggestions for your benefit.

Imagine yourself now at the top of a staircase with ten steps. With each number that I slowly count, take a step down and, with each step, you go deeper and deeper into this wonderful, desirable state of hypnosis. 10, stepping down, feeling yourself go deeper into relaxation. 9,.......8,.......7, deeper and deeper. 6, more and more relaxed. 5, more and more comfortable. 4,.......3,.......2, almost as deep as you can go, but with 1, you go yet deeper. Your body and mind are now so relaxed that you are ready to accept the suggestions you desire for your good.

Focus on your eyelids again, imagine that they are glued together and won't open. Try to open them and notice that the harder you try to open them, the more stuck they stay. Relax and stop trying. Gently open your eyes for a moment, going deeper and deeper, twice as deep as before as your eyes close. Feel your right arm getting light. It feels like it wants to float upward. Feel it getting lighter and lighter. Your arm rises. Allow it to move, notice it feels like it is rising up, up, up. When you feel upward movement, you count to three. On three, the arm plops down and you go deeper and deeper. 1 .... 2 .... 3 .... So deep, so relaxed.

Now, create a screen in your imagination. It might be a movie screen or a T.V. screen. You play out your desired outcome on this screen.

This is the induction that you can use as your basic foundation. Add your suggestions, or read your script, into the recorder. Do a separate tape for each change you want to make. The subconscious only wants to deal with one issue at a time.

REFERENCES

Blanchard, Ken, *Playing the Great Game of Golf: Making Every Minute Count*, William Morrow & Company, New York, NY, 1992.

Callahan, Tom, "Watson's Longest Yard," *Golf Digest*, June 1995.

Cohn, Patrick J., Ph.D., *The Mental Game of Golf: A Guide to Peak Performance*, Diamond Communications, Inc., South Bend, IN, 1994.

Cunningham, Les, *Hypnosport: The Creative Use of Hypnosis to Maximize Athletic Performance*, Westwood Publishing Company, Glendale, CA, 1981.

Dalloway, Marie, Ph.D., *Reflections on the Mental Side of Sports*, Optimal Performance Institute, Phoenix, AZ, 1994.

Elman, Dave, *Hypnotherapy*, Westwood Publishing Company, Glendale, CA, 1964.

Fasciana, Dr. Guy S., *Golf's Mental Magic*, Bob Adams, Inc., Holbrook, MA, 1994.

Feinstein, John, *A Good Walk Spoiled: Days and Nights on the PGA Tour*, Little, Brown and Company, Boston, MA, 1995.

Fisher, A. Garth, and John Geersten, Jr., *Golf: Your Turn for Success*, Jones and Bartlett Publishers, Boston, MA, 1992.

Gallwey, W. Timothy, *The Inner Game of Golf*, Random House, New York, NY, 1981.

Garfield, Charles A., Ph.D., *Peak Performance: Mental Training Techniques of the World's Greatest Athletes*, Warner Books, Jeremy P. Tarcher, Inc., Los Angeles, CA, 1984.

Gindes, Bernard C., M.D., *New Concepts of Hypnosis: Theories, Techniques and Practical Applications*, Wilshire Book Company, No. Hollywood, CA, 1951.

Hook, Dr. Lynne O'Neill, *Hypnotizing Yourself for Success*, R & E Publishers, Saratoga, CA.

Journal of Applied Sport Psychology, Volume 6 Number 1.

Kaloski, Bruce E., Ph.D., *The MMP Sports Improvement Training Manual*, Success Track, Garden Grove, CA, 1994.

Krasner, A. M., Ph.D., *The Wizard Within: The Krasner Method of Clinical Hypnotherapy*, American Board of Hypnotherapy Press, Santa Ana, CA, 1991.

Kriegel, Robert Ph.D., and Marilyn Harris Kriegel, Ph.D., *The C Zone: Peak Performance Under Pressure*, Ballantine Books, New York, NY, 1984.

LeCron, Leslie M., *Self-Hypnotism: The Technique and Its Use in Daily Living*, The New American Library, Inc., New York, NY, 1964.

Leonard, George, *The Ultimate Athlete*, North Atlantic Books, Berkeley, CA, 1990.

Levine, Barbara Hoberman, *Your Body Believes Every Word You Say: The Language of the Body/Mind Connection*, Aslan Publishing, Boulder Creek, CA, 1991.

Murray, Michael, *Golf in the Kingdom*, Penguin Books USA, New York, NY, 1992.

Nash, Bruce, and Allan Zullo, *The Hole Truth: Inside the Ropes of the PGA Tour*, Andrews and McMeel, Kansas City, MO, 1995.

Nicklaus, Jack, *Golf My Way*, Simon & Schuster, New York, NY, 1974.

Ostrander, Sheila, and Lynn Schroeder, *Super-Learning*, Delacorte Press/Confucian Press, New York, NY, 1979.

Ousby, William J., *The Theory and Practice of Hypnotism*, Thorsons Publishing Group, Northamptonshire, England, 1990.

Pelz, Dave, "The Amazing Truth About Putting," *Golf*, April 1995.

Penick, Harvey, *For All Who Love the Game: Lessons and Teachings for Women*, Simon & Schuster, New York, NY, 1995.

Rotella, Dr. Bob, *Golf Is Not a Game of Perfect*, Simon & Schuster, New York, NY, 1995.

Tutko, Thomas, Ph.D., and Umberto Tosi, *Sports Psyching: Playing Your Best Game All of the Time*, Jeremy P. Tarcher, Inc., Los Angeles, CA, 1976.

AUDIOCASSETTE TAPES

#1 *Side A Progressive Muscle Relaxation*
Side B Relaxation Through Visualization
This tape gives you the relaxation technique that was
developed for general muscle relaxation and insomnia.
Side B is a very effective quick stress reducer.

#2 *Side A General Golf Improvement*
Side B Overcoming First Tee Jitters
Listen to this tape and watch your game improve. You'll
also feel more comfortable teeing off.

#3 *Side A Maintaining Focus and Concentration*
Side B Mind Over Putter
Lack of concentration is the major cause of inconsistency.
Putts are the most crucial shots in a golf game. Play well
when it counts the most.

#4 *Side A Creating Confidence* (For Practice in Bed)
Side B Creating Confidence (For Listening in the Car)
Confidence is the essential emotional element for great
golf. It must be reinforced in the relaxed state and can be
reinforced while driving.

#5 *Side A Induction for Self-Hypnosis*
Side B More Inductions for Self-Hypnosis
Learn to easily put yourself in the powerful creative
hypnotic state. Use it to create breakthrough performance in any area of your life.

Tapes $15 each. All five for $70.
Applicable tax, shipping and handling will be added.
Tapes can be customized at an additional charge.

Call (800) 347-6828 to Order.

ABOUT THE AUTHOR:

Dr. Bee Epstein-Shepherd has degrees in Psychology and Personnel and Human Relations from International College, Goddard College, and the University of California Berkeley. She has had a twenty year career teaching Business Psychology and Management courses at several colleges and universities, corporate consulting, and conducting personal and professional development seminars internationally. Her interest in sport psychology developed as a result of observing the consistency of people's behavior at work and at play and recognizing that the principles of peak performance are adaptable to any activity. She is listed in numerous Who's Who Publications, including, *Who's Who of American Women* and *Who's Who in the World* and makes her home in Carmel, California.